P9-AGF-607

LIVING
AS SALT AND
LIGHT

LIVING
AS SALT AND
LIGHT

DEREK PRINCE

WHITAKER
HOUSE

Publisher's Note: This book was compiled from the extensive archive of Derek Prince's unpublished materials and approved by the Derek Prince Ministries editorial team.

Unless otherwise indicated, all Scripture quotations are taken from the *New King James Version*, © 1979, 1980, 1982, 1984 by Thomas Nelson, Inc. Used by permission. All rights reserved. Scripture quotations marked (KJV) are taken from the King James Version of the Holy Bible. The Scripture quotation marked (NIV) is taken from the *Holy Bible, New International Version*, NIV, © 1973, 1978, 1984 by the International Bible Society. Used by permission of Zondervan. All rights reserved. The Scripture quotation taken from *The Living Bible*, © 1971, is used by permission of Tyndale House Publishers, Inc., Wheaton, Illinois 60189. All rights reserved. Scripture quotations marked (NASB) are taken from the *New American Standard Bible*, NASB, © 1960, 1962, 1963, 1968, 1971, 1972, 1973, 1975, 1977 by The Lockman Foundation. Used by permission. (www.Lockman.org). The Scripture quotation marked (MOFFATT) is taken from *The Bible: James Moffatt Translation*, © 1922, 1924, 1925, 1926, 1935 by Harper Collins San Francisco; © 1950, 1952, 1953, 1954 by James A. R. Moffatt.

Boldface type in the Scripture quotations indicates the author's emphasis.

Living as Salt and Light
God's Call to Transform Your World

Derek Prince Ministries
P.O. Box 19501
Charlotte, North Carolina 28219-9501
www.derekprince.org

ISBN: 978-1-60374-899-5
eBook ISBN: 978-1-60374-900-8
Printed in the United States of America
© 2013 by Derek Prince Ministries–International

Whitaker House
1030 Hunt Valley Circle
New Kensington, PA 15068
www.whitakerhouse.com

Library of Congress Cataloging-in-Publication Data (Pending)

No part of this book may be reproduced or transmitted in any form or by any means, electronic or mechanical—including photocopying, recording, or by any information storage and retrieval system—without permission in writing from the publisher. Please direct your inquiries to permissionseditor@whitakerhouse.com.

1 2 3 4 5 6 7 8 9 10 11 🕮 19 18 17 16 15 14 13

CONTENTS

INTRODUCTION

WE CAN CHANGE THE COURSE OF NATIONAL EVENTS

In this book, we will be examining the theme of our responsibility as Christians toward the nations in which we live. It is my belief that the Word of God speaks to us about this obligation. It clearly reveals that as Christians, we are accountable for our own societies and countries. Unfortunately, the great majority of Christians have not even begun to think about this responsibility.

Many nations throughout the world are facing possibly the greatest crises of their entire history. Yours may be one of these. What a tragedy it would be if, in this context of crisis, we Christians accomplished nothing that had any bearing or positive effect upon the needs of the nations in which we live! If that were to be the case, I believe we would have failed God.

With this thought in mind, I will deal with the theme of our strategic position as Christians in our nations—including both our privileges and our responsibilities. I want to address this topic in the most useful way possible, so the teaching offered in this book will be as practical as it can be.

I once heard a speaker whose theme was the drastic situation in the United States today. He took three-quarters of his message to tell his audience how terrible conditions were, and how it was getting worse every week. As true as that might have been by itself, it certainly wasn't good news. (Let me just say that the gospel is good news. The gospel is not negative; it is positive. Jesus Christ never encountered a situation where He had to sit down, fold His hands, and say, "I'm sorry. There is nothing to be done.") At the end of his message, this speaker devoted just a little time to share his belief that a Holy Spirit revival was what was needed. I trust I am doing him justice, but I do not believe he devoted one sentence to telling us *how* we could have a Holy Spirit revival.

It is my aim in this book to point out what we can do—what lies within our power as Christians—to change the course of national events for the better. I am firmly convinced that our countries need to be changed and can be changed. I am also convinced that *we* are the people who must bring about that change. My goal will be to show you from the Word of God how we can accomplish it.

PART I

OUR POSITION, PRIVILEGE, AND RESPONSIBILITY IN THE WORLD

CHAPTER 1

A CITY ON A HILL—THE ONLY LIGHT

The Sermon on the Mount is universally accepted by Christians as the measure of faith and life that Jesus set for all true believers. It is not a special message just for those who have leadership roles, such as teachers, apostles, prophets, evangelists, or preachers. In this passage of Scripture, Jesus revealed the will of God, or God's standard, which applies to every faithful Christian. The message known as the Sermon on the Mount is unfolded in three chapters, Matthew 5–7.

For our opening text, I would like to present what Jesus said in Matthew 5:13–14:

> You are the salt of the earth; but if the salt loses its flavor, how shall it be seasoned? It is then good for nothing but to be thrown out and trampled underfoot by men. You are the light of the world. A city that is set on a hill cannot be hidden.

Speaking to all Christians, Jesus told us three very important facts about ourselves: we are the salt of the earth, the light of the world, and a city that is set on a hill and cannot be hidden. As an introduction to my theme, I want to take a little time to point out some of the self-evident implications of these three statements. We will take them in the reverse order in which they were spoken. In chapter 1 of this book, we will cover the first two statements, and in chapter 2 the third statement.

A CITY SET ON A HILL

First of all, we are *"a city that is set on a hill [and] cannot be hidden"* (Mark 5:13). This fact is true of every person who publicly professes faith in Jesus Christ as Savior and Lord. The moment you make that profession publicly, you become a city that is set on a hill. You cannot be hidden. You are conspicuous: eyes will be on you from every direction, at all times, whether you are attending school or working at a factory or in an office. These eyes will be turned in your direction to see if your Christianity is real. What will those watching you be asking themselves? *Is your faith genuine? Do you truly believe what you claim to believe? Do you live it out?*

People will analyze every aspect of your life—your family life, your business life, your social life, and so forth. They will also analyze the conduct and testimony of the church you attend. In most cases, they will form their judgment of Christianity from what they see in you. You are a city that is set on a hill.

I tell you frankly that as a young man in the Anglican Church in Great Britain, I came to the conclusion that Christianity was a failure. I formed my opinion by looking at the people around me and deciding they did not really believe what they claimed to believe.

So, you must realize that the moment you profess faith in Jesus Christ, you become conspicuous. You cannot avoid this reality. If you don't want to be conspicuous; if you don't want to be watched, judged, and analyzed; then don't profess faith in Jesus Christ. But if you profess faith in Jesus Christ, that will be your situation—people will begin observing you. From that time on, you will be a city that is set on a hill and cannot be hidden.

THE LIGHT OF THE WORLD

Second, Jesus said, *"You are the light of the world"* (Matthew 5:14). At various times and places in my life, I have been a teacher of the English language, and I understand English well enough to know that when the Scripture says *"You are the light of the world,"* it means that we are *the* light. In other words, there is no other light. The word *"the"* used here is exclusive. We are the *only* light. The world has no other light.

Jesus declared, *"As long as I am in the world, I am the light of the world"* (John 9:5). But now that He is not physically in the world, we are His representatives. Therefore, in His place, *we* are the light of the world. If we do not give light, there is no other source to which the world can turn or look for light. This means that *the world is totally dependent upon Christians for light.*

There is a simple illustration in the Old Testament that teaches us how significant we are as the light of the world. In the tabernacle that God commanded Moses to build, there were two compartments. The first was called the Holy Place, and the second was called the Holiest of All, or the Holy of Holies. In the Holy Place, there were only three objects of furniture. One of them was the golden altar of incense, and it was placed immediately in front of the second veil, which was the way into the Holiest of All. No one could go into the Holiest of All unless he held a censer filled with incense from the golden altar.

IF WE DO NOT GIVE LIGHT, THERE IS NO OTHER SOURCE TO WHICH THE WORLD CAN TURN OR LOOK FOR LIGHT.

That leaves two other items of furniture in the Holy Place. On the left-hand side was a seven-branched candlestick. On the right-hand side, opposite the candlestick, was the table of showbread. The writer of Hebrews told us that these items were symbolic—they contained a message to the church of Jesus Christ. (See Hebrews 9.)

Let's look first at what the candlestick says to us. In Scripture, the candlestick always typifies the church. It had seven branches, typifying the sevenfold nature of the church, begotten by the Spirit of God. (The same sevenfold message is represented by the seven churches of Asia referred to in chapters 2 and 3 of the book of Revelation.)

We would be wrong to picture this candlestick as the same kind we have today—wax candles standing firmly in some kind of base. In the tabernacle, the "candles" were bowls with channels filled with oil. Little wicks were dipped in the oil, and the light was produced by igniting the wick, which set the oil in the wick on fire. Unless there was oil in the candles, and unless that oil was ignited, the candles gave no light. And, in the Holy Place, the candlestick was the only source of light. If there was no light coming from the candlestick, there was no light at all.

Do you see how this is true of the church? We, too, are the *only* light. There is no other light. We are the seven-branched candlestick. We give light only when we are filled with oil and when the oil in us is set on fire.

In Scripture, oil is always a type of the Holy Spirit. This symbolism tells us that the church can give light only when it is filled with the Holy Spirit and set on fire by God. The candlestick, in itself, was incapable of producing light without the oil and without the fire. Considering this fact, we are reminded that John the Baptist said of Jesus, *"He will baptize you with the Holy Spirit and fire"* (Matthew 3:11; Luke 3:16).

OUR MAIN PURPOSE AS LIGHT

The function of the candlestick was to cast light on the object that was immediately opposite it, which was the golden table of showbread. The showbread, of course, represents Jesus Christ, who said,

> *I am the bread of life....I am the living bread which came down from heaven. If anyone eats of this bread, he will live forever; and the bread that I shall give is My flesh, which I shall give for the life of the world.*　　　　　(John 6:48, 51)

The whole purpose of the candlestick was to do one thing and one thing only: to illuminate the table of showbread. This is exactly true of the church of Jesus Christ. We are here on earth for one purpose and one purpose only: to cast light on Jesus, the Bread of Life. And we do this only when we are filled with the Holy Spirit and set on fire by God.

Here we have a remarkable picture of the church. Apart from the candlestick, there was no source of light in the Holy Place. Apart from the church, there is no light in the world. Just as the candlestick can give light only when it is filled with oil and set on fire, the church can give light only when it is filled with the Holy Spirit and set on fire. The candlestick had only one object upon which to cast light—the table of showbread. The church has only one "object" upon which to cast light—the Lord Jesus Christ.

The only reason that you and I, as Christians, are here is to cast light on Jesus Christ, the Bread of Life. This is the primary purpose of our presence on the earth. Everything else we may do is secondary to that. We are the light of the world.

CHAPTER 2

THE SALT OF THE EARTH

In the previous chapter, we introduced Jesus' description of the church, which He gave in a message known as the Sermon on the Mount, recorded in Matthew 5:13–14. We are "a city that is set on a hill," which the eyes of the world are carefully watching. We are also "the light"—the only light—that illuminates Christ to a dying world.

In this chapter, we focus on our third role: we are "the salt of the earth." Again, the word "the" is exclusive. It means that the earth has no other salt—we are the only salt available to the earth. There are various ways in which you can apply the significance of salt. However, since I am not a scientist, I will keep my explanations on a very humble plane. Let me just point out certain obvious facts about salt.

SALT GIVES FLAVOR

One great function of salt is to give flavor to that which would otherwise lack it. In Job 6:6, the Scriptures record Job as saying, *"Can flavorless food be eaten without salt? Or is there any taste in the white of an egg?"* The answer is no. That is why, when you eat the white of an egg, if you are like me, you sprinkle salt on it to give it flavor.

In the same way, Christians are the salt of the earth. We are here to give the earth flavor in the sight of God. Apart from our presence on the earth, there is no reason why God should deal with this world in grace and mercy any longer. We are the only factor that makes the earth acceptable to Him, the only restraint that holds back His final judgment and wrath on a Christ-rejecting world. As long we are on the earth, our responsibility is to live in such a way that we commend this earth to God.

FOR TEN GRAINS OF SALT

In Genesis 18, we read how the Lord stopped at the home of Abraham on His way to the city of Sodom. The Lord told Abraham what He was planning—He had come to bring judgment upon that city. Abraham was very concerned about what God had told him, because his nephew, Lot, as well as Lot's family, lived in Sodom. So, Abraham walked with the Lord toward Sodom, boldly pleading with Him to spare that wicked city. He "bargained" with the Lord (if I may use that term) on the basis of numbers, saying, in effect, "Lord, if there were fifty righteous men in that city, would You spare it?" The Lord said yes.

Then Abraham said, "If there were forty, would You spare the city?" The Lord said yes.

Abraham said, "If there were thirty, would You spare the city?" The Lord said yes.

Abraham said, "If there were twenty, would You spare the city?" The Lord said yes.

Then Abraham said, "Please, Lord, do not be angry, but I want to ask once more. If there were just ten righteous men in that city, would You spare it for the sake of the ten righteous men that are in it?" The Lord said, "Yes, I would." The tragedy is that the Lord did not find ten righteous men in Sodom.

Whenever I read this story, I cannot help but wonder whether Abraham did a little mental calculation. Could he have said to himself, *There are my nephew and his wife, and his unmarried daughters, and his married daughters… between them, surely, wouldn't they be able to muster up ten righteous people?* And if Lot had been doing his job, they probably would have equaled that number. But Lot was one of those believers who failed God. Oh, he was a believer, all right. He had heard all the revelations from Abraham, but he was not living in the light of that revelation.

A certain thought always touches me when I hear the story of Lot. I share it especially with you if you are a parent. When I think of the terrible responsibility of Lot, I ask myself, *Who took the family into Sodom?* The answer, of course, is Lot. He took them in, but he could not get them out again. He escaped with just two daughters—ultimately, not even his wife got out. When she looked back at the city, which was contrary to God's instructions, she turned into a pillar of salt.

Likewise, if you are a parent, you can take your children and other family members into situations that you cannot get them out of—and you will be held accountable. It is a most sobering thought. I cannot picture how Lot must have felt when he looked at the blazing, smoking ruins of Sodom and knew that his own married daughters and his sons-in-law had perished, not to mention any grandchildren they may have given him. And I wonder if he looked at the pillar of salt, which had been his wife, and said to himself, *I took them there.*

OUR RESPONSIBILITY IS TO LIVE IN SUCH A WAY THAT WE COMMEND THIS EARTH TO GOD.

Do you really understand that you can lead people into situations that you can't get them out of? I hear people make statements like this: "Well, the Word of God is not being proclaimed in this particular church, but we stay there for the sake of the children." My response to this attitude is, "So, what is not good enough for you is good enough for your children?"

Friend, you need to take more serious heed to your children. Don't imagine that your children can be fooled with second best—they can't. Young people today are discerning and discriminating. They look deeply at matters, and they take measure of them. Do you know what they want? Above all else, they want honesty and reality. If they don't see it, they won't buy it. You cannot fool them, so don't try. Don't be like Lot, because you could live to regret it eternally.

OUR PRESENCE MAKES A DIFFERENCE

We derive an eternal principle in the example of Lot. For ten righteous men, God would have spared an entire city. That proportion is applicable today as well. Ten grains of salt can commend a whole serving to God. As I said earlier, our business is to be such that we commend this earth to Him. Our presence makes a difference. Our presence causes God to deal with the world in a way that He otherwise would not.

Every believer should be a single grain of salt in the particular place God has put him. God does not lump all believers together in one place, any more than we would put all the salt we are to consume at a particular meal into just one mouthful. It would taste bitter! Along with all believers, you have been scattered to a particular place in order to be a grain of salt to flavor the world—whether that place is in your family, at your school, at your place of employment, or anywhere else.

You may say, "I feel so lonely there." But you are there for a purpose. You are there to give flavor to a place that, without you, would have no flavor at all.

I was saved and baptized in the Holy Spirit during the Second World War when I was a soldier in the British Army. God did not take me out of the army and say, "Now that you are a Christian, this ungodly atmosphere and these ungodly surroundings are no good for you. So, I will exchange that dirty brown uniform you have for a fine black suit with a round white collar, and I will put you in a nice ecclesiastical, academic atmosphere where you can really flourish as a Christian."

Do you know what the Lord said to me instead? "In the same barrack room where you cursed, drank, and blasphemed, I am going to show what it means to be a Christian. My grace is sufficient for you."

Someone once shared with me the following beautiful thought: "The will of God will never place you where the grace of God cannot keep you." That truth bears repeating: The will of God will never place you where the grace of God cannot keep you. Wherever you are, if you are in the will of God, His grace is sufficient for you.

Oh, how I thank God for the army! Prior to my service, I had a very prolonged and elaborate education. But the most useful part of my education was in the British Army. It was certainly not the most enjoyable, but it was the most useful. (My first wife, Lydia, always said that she was glad she didn't meet me until I came out of the army.) I am mentioning my army experience for a reason—my presence in my unit made a difference.

For about six months after I was saved and baptized in the Holy Spirit, I was in the North African desert in the midst of the North African theater of World War II. I was with a medical unit as a medical orderly, and, for a time, we were cut off behind enemy lines. We got lost in the desert—which is very easy to do. For about twenty-four hours, we didn't know whether we were going to be taken prisoner or find our way back to safety. In that situation, a very tough truck driver, who cursed and blasphemed and lived a godless life, came to me and said, in all sincerity, "Corporal Prince, I am glad you are with us." He was sensible enough to know that my presence made a difference—and it did. I was with that particular company for two years in the desert, and they never lost a man. After I left them, they lost many men.

EACH OF US HAS BEEN SCATTERED TO A PARTICULAR PLACE IN ORDER TO BE A GRAIN OF SALT TO FLAVOR THE WORLD.

As Christians, we are like grains of salt. Our presence makes a difference. There should not be a single believer among us whose presence fails to make a difference.

Toward the end of the war, I was put in charge of the admissions office of a hospital on the Mount of Olives, and a young lance corporal was assigned to work with me. For the first two weeks or so, for some reason or other, I never spoke directly to him about God or religion. One day, another soldier came by, and as these two were talking in front of me, the lance corporal who had been working with me began to blaspheme. Suddenly, he checked himself, blushed bright red, turned around, and said to me, "I'm sorry, Corporal Prince, I didn't know you were here. I wouldn't have spoken like that." I had never told him that I disapproved of cursing or blaspheming. I had not actually spoken to him about God. But my presence convicted him that it was wrong.

That is what it means to be salt. If you do not make an impact where you live, something is wrong. If people carry on just as they were carrying on anyhow, even though you are there, something is wrong with your life as a Christian.

SALT IS A POWERFUL PRESERVATIVE

Another great feature of salt is that it is a preservative. Before the days of refrigeration, when people went on long journeys and wanted to preserve their meat, they salted it. The salt had the effect of holding back the forces of corruption that would otherwise have worked in the meat.

Likewise, since we are the salt of the earth, we are here to hold back the forces of corruption. As long as we are in the earth, the forces of evil that are at work—godlessness, rebellion, and so forth—will not be allowed to come to their fullness. Only after the church has been taken from the earth will wickedness come to its final culmination. We are here to arrest and hold back the forces of corruption—whether they are forces affecting the moral realm, the social realm, the political realm, or any other realm of the society in which we live. We are responsible to hold those forces back because we are the salt of the earth.

If our presence does not commend the earth to God and cause Him to act differently toward the world than He would if we were not here, and if our presence does not hold back the forces of corruption, do you know what we have become? We have become salt that has lost its flavor. As a result, we are salt that is not doing its job. We are salt that has become "saltless."

Recall what Jesus said about salt that has lost its flavor: "*It is then good for nothing but to be thrown out and trampled underfoot by men*" (Matthew 5:13). In just about every case, the term "good-for-nothing" is one of the worst remarks you can make about somebody. To be a good-for-nothing is just about as bad as you can be—and that is what the church is if it is not doing its job. We are good for nothing except for one thing: "*...to be thrown out and trampled underfoot by men.*"

I want you to note that in the Sermon on the Mount, Jesus warned us that it is *men's* feet that will trample the saltless church. God will use men to do it. If you consider what is happening in the world today, you will see millions of feet just waiting to trample us under. There is no exaggeration in that statement.

Hordes of enemies around the world would consider it a privilege to trample us underfoot. If we do not change, they will do it. And, when we are being trampled, we will have no cause for complaint. All we will be able to say is, "We deserve it...and God warned us." The bitterest reflection of all will be that it never needed to happen. All we have to do is repent and change our ways. It does not need to happen.

AN OPPORTUNITY TO RESPOND

I am absolutely convinced that the church of Jesus Christ, in every part of the world, could rise to the occasion and meet God's very simple, very clear, very specific condition. If we would do so, we could change and then arrest the downward course of events. On the other hand, if we don't do so, it will be our fault, and we will be the ones who will suffer first and worst. If we suffer for our failure to meet God's condition, we deserve it.

Before we go any further in this book, allow me to give a simple application to what we have covered thus far. If you are not convinced by what I have presented, by all means, don't feel compelled to respond. But if you believe that what I have expounded to you in a practical way is what the Scriptures teach, I invite you to read Matthew 5:13 again:

You are the salt of the earth; but if the salt loses its flavor, how shall it be seasoned? It is then good for nothing but to be thrown out and trampled underfoot by men.

I want to make the above verse very personal for you right now so that you can apply Jesus' statement to your life. We realize that Jesus is talking to Christians, and we are Christians. Therefore, where it says "*You...*" I want you read it as "*We....*" And, in the middle of the verse, where it says, "*It is then good for nothing,*" I want you to read, "*We are then good for nothing.*" I believe this change is absolutely legitimate.

After you say the following, you are going to be answerable to God in time and eternity for what you have said. So, if you are ready, try it now, out loud:

We are the salt of the earth; but if the salt loses its flavor, how shall it be seasoned? We are then good for nothing but to be thrown out and trampled underfoot by men.

CHAPTER 3

OUR WRESTLING MATCH

We continue now in our study of the position, privilege, and responsibility God has given us as Christians. In this chapter, I am going to concentrate on the major scriptural reason why the church alone, of all the agencies in the earth today, has the ability to change the world situation effectively for the better.

DRAFTED INTO SPIRITUAL WARFARE

To understand this truth, let us look at Ephesians 6:12. I believe all commentators would agree that in this verse, where Paul said *"we,"* he was speaking about all Christians. He was not talking about some special class of people but about Christians in general, including you and me. This is what he said:

> *For we do not wrestle against flesh and blood, but against principalities, against powers, against the rulers of the darkness of this age, against spiritual hosts of wickedness in the heavenly places.*
>
> (Ephesians 6:12)

I have studied Greek since I was ten years old, and I would like to reword this verse in a way that adheres to the original meaning and makes it more vivid:

For we do not wrestle against flesh and blood, but against principalities, or rulerships; against powers, or authorities; against the world rulers of the present darkness; against spirits of lawlessness in heavenly places, or the heavenlies.

(Before reading further, please read the above statement again, because it bears repetition.)

First of all, notice that as Christians, we are engaged in a wrestling match. This is not a situation in which we have another option. If we are Christians, we wrestle. We have no choice in the matter. It is necessary. When you become a Christian, you automatically become involved in a tremendous spiritual conflict.

I believe this picture of wrestling, which Paul took from the ancient Olympic Games, is particularly significant. Why? Because wrestling is the most intensive, the most exacting, the most all-inclusive of all struggles. It demands the total person in total effort. And that is exactly how it is in the spiritual realm: It is a total conflict—with spirit, soul, and body all involved in a mighty battle against unseen spiritual forces in the heavenly realm.

SPIRIT, SOUL, AND BODY ARE ALL INVOLVED IN A MIGHTY BATTLE AGAINST UNSEEN SPIRITUAL FORCES IN THE HEAVENLY REALM.

Please note the emphasis that we are not fighting human beings, or people of flesh and blood. We are not fighting some person at work, or a fellow Christian, or a political opponent, or even the dictator of some foreign nation. Our fight is not with human personalities. We are fighting spiritual forces, spiritual personalities. They are persons, but they are spirit persons—*"persons without bodies"* (Ephesians 6:12 TLB).

These spirit persons exist in an unseen realm; it is not visible to the natural eye. Nevertheless, their realm is absolutely real—in fact, more real than the visible world. The apostle Paul said, *"The things which are seen are temporary, but the things which are not seen are eternal"* (2 Corinthians 4:18). The things that we can see are temporal.

They are transient; they are impermanent. But the things in the unseen spiritual realm are permanent. The visible, temporary things will pass away. The unseen, spiritual, eternal things will continue.

THE WHOLE WORLD LIES UNDER SATAN'S INFLUENCE

We see from Ephesians 6:12 that we are engaged in a tremendous wrestling match against unseen forces that dictate and control the course of world affairs from a position in the heavenly places. This is what the Word of God says. As we read in 1 John 5:19, *"...the whole world lies under the sway of the wicked one."*

The King James Version translates this phrase as *"...the whole world lieth in wickedness,"* but a more accurate translation is "the whole world lies in the *wicked one.*" In other words, the whole world is in the lap of Satan, or the devil. He is the world ruler. He and the forces that join him in rebellion against God are the world rulers of this present darkness. Paul brought out this fact in Ephesians 2. Speaking to Christians, he said:

> *And you He made alive, who were dead in trespasses and sins, in which you once walked according to the course of this world, according to the prince of the power of the air, the spirit who now works in the sons of disobedience, among whom also we all once conducted ourselves in the lusts of our flesh, fulfilling the desires of the flesh and of the mind, and were by nature children of wrath, just as the others.*
>
> (Ephesians 2:1–3)

Paul stated that until we came to Jesus Christ and were converted, we were in the same condition as all the other unredeemed people throughout the world. We were under the control of *"the prince of the power of the air"*—the spirit of the air, or the spirit of the authority of the air. *"Prince of the power of the air"* is one of the titles of Satan, who works in all of unregenerate, unconverted, disobedient humanity. He dominates and controls people through the lusts of the flesh and of the mind.

Please note that Satan dominates the rebellious intellectual just as much as he dominates the prostitute or the alcoholic. He dominates and controls all unconverted, unregenerate humanity by unseen spiritual forces that control their minds and their fleshly lusts. Not only is Satan called *"the prince of the power of the air,"* but he is also called *"the prince* ["ruler" NKJV] *of this world"*—Jesus called him that three times. (See John 12:31 KJV; 14:30 KJV; 16:11 KJV.) He is the *"god of this world,"* as the apostle Paul described him in 2 Corinthians 4:4 (KJV).

DEALING WITH SATAN AND HIS FORCES

This great ruler of the unseen forces of darkness has deployed innumerable multitudes of evil spirits, which are all working under his control against God and against the welfare of the human race. As Christians, you and I are called to deal with Satan and with the forces that work with him.

BEHIND THE SOCIAL SITUATIONS, ECONOMIC SITUATIONS, POLITICAL SITUATIONS, AND INTERNATIONAL SITUATIONS ARE UNSEEN SPIRITUAL FORCES.

How did this situation of spiritual conflict come about? First, by Satan's rebellion in heaven; and second, by man's rebellion on earth. Humankind has become the subject and slave of Satan—not through God's ordinance but through man's rebellion. Man sided with Satan against God and thus made himself subject to Satan. Until we understand this reality, we cannot understand the true situation in the world today.

So, behind the seen realm is the unseen realm. Behind the forces we are familiar with and that the newspapers report to us daily—social situations, economic situations, political situations, international situations, and so forth—behind all these circumstances, dominating them, controlling them, and directing them, are unseen spiritual forces. Clearly, they are directing them all toward evil; toward rebellion against God and toward destruction. Yet it is your privilege and mine, your responsibility and mine, to intervene and change this situation.

CHAPTER 4

THE ENEMY WE BATTLE

In the previous chapter, we talked about Satan's behind-the-scenes role in which he manipulates and dominates world events and the human race. Now, we will examine his role more closely. Unless we understand our enemy, we will not be able to battle him effectively.

There is an account in the Old Testament that lifts a little corner of the veil separating us from the spiritual realm and shows us the reality of the unseen evil spiritual powers controlling the destiny of nations. In the first part of Ezekiel 28, we are introduced to two persons. The first person is called *"the prince of Tyre* [the city of Tyrus]" (verse 2), and the second person is called *"the king of Tyre"* (verse 12). These two persons were related in the following way: The prince of Tyre was the visible human ruler of Tyre. But the king of Tyre was the invisible satanic personality dominating the visible ruler—and through him, the entire city and empire of Tyre. Indeed, when you analyze what these verses say about the king of Tyre, there is only person to whom this description could possibly apply—Satan. There is no other person in the universe of whom these words in Ezekiel 28 could be true.

We will first examine what is said about the prince of Tyre, and then we will move our focus to the king of Tyre. Understand that this is a historical prophecy relating to a historical situation in the past. But it is also a God-given glimpse of a situation yet to come in the world under the dominion of the Antichrist. The Antichrist will be the last great evil ruler who will come to dominate and rule all nations immediately prior to the return of Jesus Christ, who will then set up His earthly kingdom. The descriptions in Ezekiel of the prince of Tyre and the king of Tyre are the clearest single previews anywhere in Scripture of the Antichrist and how Satan will rule the world through him.

Please keep these patterns in mind, because there is much in Ezekiel 28 that immediately leads to the prophecy of the Antichrist in the New Testament, as I will point out briefly. Now, in examining this chapter, we find these words:

> Son of man, say to the prince of Tyre, "Thus says the Lord GOD: 'Because your heart is lifted up, and you say, "I am a god, I sit in the seat of gods, in the midst of the seas," yet you are a man, and not a god, though you set your heart as the heart of a god (Behold, you are wiser than Daniel! There is no secret that can be hidden from you!...).'"
>
> (Ezekiel 28:2–3)

To be wiser than Daniel is to be pretty wise. It is important to notice that Satan can make a man even wiser than Daniel. The passage continues:

> "'(With your wisdom and your understanding you have gained riches for yourself, and gathered gold and silver into your treasuries...).Will you still say before him who slays you, "I am a god"? But you shall be a man, and not a god, in the hand of him who slays you.'"
>
> (Ezekiel 28:4, 9)

How clear the Scripture is. Here is a man, obviously a human being, who claims to be a god and portrays himself as a god. But he is not God, nor is he a spirit being. He is a man, a being of flesh and blood—one who is mortal and who is going to die an unnatural death. He will be killed by the sword.

Let us now move on to the king of Tyre, the unseen personality behind this man. Notice what is said about him:

Son of man, take up a lamentation for the king of Tyre, and say to him, "Thus says the Lord GOD: 'You were the seal of perfection, full of wisdom and perfect in beauty.'" (Ezekiel 28:12)

This is a picture of Satan as he was before he fell. Verse 13 says, *"You were in Eden* [notice that], *the garden of God."* The earthly ruler of Tyre had never been near Eden, the garden of God. Eden had been blotted out centuries before this passage was written. Verse 13 then describes all the beautiful stones with which the "king of Tyre" was adorned. Please don't imagine that Eve was deceived by some slimy, slithering serpent. She wasn't. Whatever this being was, he was gorgeous—very beautiful and very elegant. It was only *after* he deceived Adam and Eve that he was cursed and destined to go upon his belly as a snake. (See Genesis 3:14.)

Ezekiel 28:14 says, *"You were the anointed cherub who covers."* So, we see where Satan was. Until he fell, he was the cherub that covered God's throne.

Continuing on, we read:

You were on the holy mountain of God; you walked back and forth in the midst of fiery stones. You were perfect in your ways from the day you were created, till iniquity was found in you. (Ezekiel 28:14–15)

Verse 17 adds, *"Your heart was lifted up because of your beauty."*

Why did Satan fall? Because of pride in his own beauty.

LUCIFER: THE FALSE DAWN

In Isaiah 14, we read another enlightening description of the fall of Satan. It begins with this statement in verse 12: *"How you are fallen from heaven, O Lucifer, son of the morning!"*

I want to tell you a secret. I learned something in the North African desert that confirms these verses in which we are told the original name of Satan—*"Lucifer,"* which means "the morning star." For about nine months in the desert campaign, we had no lights, we saw no paved roads, and we lived, ate, and slept on the sand. We went to bed when the sun set, and we got up when the sun rose. During those nights in the desert,

I discovered that at certain seasons of the year, there is a false dawn. That is to say, the morning star comes up over the horizon immediately preceding the sun. It is so bright that it causes the whole horizon to be illuminated and to glow. You would really imagine that the sun was coming up; instead, this unusually, unnaturally bright star comes up. A little while later, the real sun comes up. Let me assure you, when the true sun rises, you see no more of the morning star, because it is obscured in the brilliance of the sun's rays.

This is a picture of what will happen in the world with the Antichrist. He is going to bring humanity a false dawn immediately before the coming of the true *"Sun of Righteousness"* (Malachi 4:2)—Jesus Christ. This tremendous ruler will arise and say, "I'll bring peace and prosperity and order. I'll solve your problems." He will be just like the morning star. He will be so bright that when he comes up on the horizon, people will think, *This is the real sun*. But when Jesus Christ comes, you will see no more of the Antichrist.

In the book of Revelation, Jesus is called *"the Bright and Morning Star"* (Revelation 22:16). Understand that this phrase refers to the sun. It does not refer to "the morning star," or Lucifer. It is very important to be clear about this. Lucifer is what we call "the morning star." But Jesus is the sun itself, *"the Bright and Morning Star."*

REBELLION: THE ROOT OF SIN

What was Lucifer's motivation in going against God? Why did he fall? We have seen that he fell because of pride. The next two verses in Isaiah 14 give us additional insight into why he was cut down:

> For you have said in your heart: "I will ascend into heaven, I will exalt my throne above the stars of God; I will also sit on the mount of the congregation on the farthest sides of the north; I will ascend above the heights of the clouds, I will be like the Most High." (Isaiah 14:13–14)

Did you notice one phrase that is repeated five times in this passage? "I will." That is the basis of sin—it is "I will." It is the rebellious "I" set against God.

Sin is like a tree: it has roots, a trunk, and branches. Most preaching and church activity is concerned with only the branches of sin—things like smoking, drinking, swearing, and gambling. Even the trunk, out of which comes sin, is not where sin originates. The origin of sin is the "self," the "I will," set in rebellion against God. It is the root of sin.

Just before Jesus came to John the Baptist to be baptized and begin His earthly ministry, John told the religious leaders of the day, *"Even now the ax is laid to the root of the trees"* (Matthew 3:10; Luke 3:9). The New Testament was radical. *Radical* means "it goes to the root." Laying the ax to the root is the most radical dealing of God with any age or dispensation.

THE ANTICHRIST IS GOING TO BRING HUMANITY A FALSE DAWN IMMEDIATELY BEFORE THE COMING OF THE TRUE "SUN OF RIGHTEOUSNESS."

Jesus said, *"If any man will come after me, let him deny himself"* (Matthew 16:24 kjv). That statement describes the first step— cutting off the "root" of self. You cannot be a Christian until you have denied self. Very simply, to deny oneself means to say no to self. The old ego says, "I want." Therefore, you say, "No, Christ wants. I will not please myself. I am not here to do my own will. My Savior is the Son of God who came to do the will of His Father who sent Him. Likewise, I am a son of God, and I came to do the will of Him who sent me."

The first step to the Christian life, then, is self-denial. We have lots of miserable people in our churches whose lives are full of failure because they have not dealt with the root. Most of them are fiddling around with a few top branches.

So, here we have the root of rebellion exposed as the ego that promotes itself and resists God. Remember, this root didn't start on earth. It started in heaven with Lucifer's *"I will."* Five times, Lucifer set his will against God. That is rebellion, the basic nature of sin. Note Lucifer's last statement in Isaiah 14:14: *"'I will be like the Most High.'* I will be equal with God." That is exactly the rebellious idea that Satan, as the adversary, employed to tempt Eve. He said, "If you eat of this tree, you will be like God." (See Genesis 3:5.)

In contrast, the book of Philippians says this about Jesus' mind-set: "[Jesus], *although He existed in the form of God, did not regard equality with God a thing to be grasped, but emptied Himself, taking the form of a bond-servant, and being made in the likeness of men*" (Philippians 2:6–7 NASB). Jesus did not consider equality with God something to be grabbed at. Satan grabbed at it, but Jesus did not have to. It was His by divine, eternal right. That is the difference.

The root of all problems in the world is the rebellion that is working in the *"children of disobedience"* (Ephesians 2:2 KJV). Behind that disobedience is a prince of rebellion in the unseen realm who is dominating and controlling all the children of rebellion.

Another confirmation of this truth is found in 2 Thessalonians. In this passage, we see how perfectly Ezekiel 28 reflects what Paul wrote:

> *Let no one deceive you by any means; for that Day will not come unless the falling away comes first, and the man of sin* [the correct translation is *"man of lawlessness"* (NIV, NASB), or "rebellion"] *is revealed, the son of perdition, who opposes and exalts himself above all that is called God or that is worshipped, so that he sits as God in the temple of God, showing himself that he is God.*   (2 Thessalonians 2:3–4)

Remember the prince of Tyre? He said, *"I am a god"* (Ezekiel 28:2). But God said, in effect, "You are a man, and you will die like a man." So, we have seen the type and the antitype, the Old Testament and the New. But behind all of this is the truth that the unseen evil spirit world dominates all those who are still *"children of disobedience"* (Ephesians 2:2 KJV) and therefore *"children of wrath"* (verse 3).

CHAPTER 5

TAKING THE INITIATIVE

Our previous chapter lifted the veil on the origins of Satan and of his strategies and tactics. In this chapter, we will uncover a principle of spiritual warfare that will provide the reason for some of the delays and challenges we have encountered in our walk of faith. When we understand this principle, we will be better able to fulfill our responsibility to be salt and light in the world.

The principle may be found in the story of what the prophet Daniel encountered in the way of spiritual opposition. This narrative begins with a simple statement from Daniel: *"In those days I, Daniel, was mourning three full weeks"* (Daniel 10:2). Daniel was devoting himself for three weeks to special prayer and fasting in order to more effectively seek God. At the end of three weeks, the answer to Daniel's prayer came in the form of a visitation from the archangel Gabriel.

> *Then he* [Gabriel] *said to me, "Do not fear, Daniel, for from the first day that you set your heart to understand, and to humble yourself before your God, your words were heard; and I have come because of your words."* (Daniel 10:12)

Daniel's prayer was heard the first day, but the answer came on the twenty-first day. Why did he have to wait three weeks? Here is the reason Gabriel gave:

> But the prince of the kingdom of Persia withstood me twenty-one days; and behold, Michael, one of the chief princes, came to help me, for I had been left alone there with the kings of Persia. (Daniel 10:13)

Note that "the prince of the kingdom of Persia" was not a human being; it was the spirit ruler behind the earthly kingdom of Persia. When Daniel started to pray for the restoration of Israel from its captivity (which was closely connected with the Persian Empire), and God immediately responded by sending the angel Gabriel with the answer to Daniel, this unseen evil power withstood Gabriel in the heavenly realm for twenty-one days.

THE INITIATIVE LIES WITH US

Are you beginning to understand why the answer to your prayer sometimes tarries? Can you see that just like Daniel, you are involved in a spiritual war? The above account points to a tremendously important fact: It was Daniel's prayer on earth that got the angels moving in heaven.

Friend, the initiative is with the church; it is *not* with the angels. Outcomes depend on what *we* do. The angels are *"ministering spirits, sent forth to minister for them who shall be heirs of salvation"* (Hebrews 1:14 KJV). We are not waiting for the angels; the angels are waiting for us.

When you begin to pray, you stir the angels up—and not only the good angels but also the bad ones whose rule you are disrupting. Maybe you have started to discover how true this is! Notice that it was Daniel's prayers that opened the way for the angel Gabriel to come.

Do you understand what we have to do?

In relation to spiritual warfare, most Christians picture themselves as little mice—poor, weak, timorous, cowardly, sleepy mice, disturbed out of their nest, just hoping to get back again as quickly as possible. Friend, we are the rulers! We are the people with the initiative. The world is waiting for us—both the unseen world and the seen world. We are the people who ultimately decide the destiny of nations. We are the salt of the earth; we are the light of the world.

We must realize that we are not unimportant. We are the most important people in the world today. You can't be a Christian without being important. You matter—outcomes depend on you. For too long, you have been waiting for somebody else to do something about the problems of the world.

The church has had this attitude through the centuries: "Well, if Satan attacks, maybe I can hold out." It's about time we stop waiting for Satan to take the initiative, and instead take the initiative against him. It's about time we give Satan the impression that if the church attacks, *he* will not be able to hold out. We must take action, and this age will not close until we do. It depends on us.

BEHIND THE SCENES

Let us look at one more insight from the story of Daniel that we must understand. As the angel was leaving Daniel, he said, *"Do you know why I have come to you? And now I must return to fight with the prince of Persia; and when I have gone forth, indeed the prince of Greece will come"* (Daniel 10:20). The next great empire after Persia was Greece. Behind each of these empires was an unseen spirit personality called the *"prince"* of the empire of Persia and the *"prince"* of the empire of Greece.

There was war in the heavenly realm in order to open the way for Israel, God's scattered people in exile, to return to their inheritance. Both the kingdom of Persia and the kingdom of Greece were involved. Behind all that took place in the historical, political realm was this unseen conflict in the spiritual realm. In that conflict, the prayers of God's people on earth were decisive.

The same principle is absolutely true today. The unseen spiritual realm decides the course of history. It decides the political, social, and economic outcomes. The spiritual realm is where the issues are settled—and the pivotal factor in settling those issues is the church of Jesus Christ on earth.

CHRIST OPERATES THROUGH HIS BODY

There is another major reason why we are the salt of the earth and the light of the world. As Scripture clearly states, we are the body of Jesus Christ (see, for example, Ephesians 1:22–23), and Jesus Christ operates through His body. God will not set aside His Son Jesus Christ, because it would be dishonoring to Him. Likewise, He will not set aside the church, which is the body of His Son. In His sovereignty, God has limited Himself to doing through the church the most important acts that need to be done. And "the church" means you and me.

WE ARE THE PEOPLE WHO ULTIMATELY DECIDE THE DESTINY OF NATIONS.

I trust you are beginning to realize this truth: *you matter.* It always grieves me to hear Christians talking about themselves as though they are insignificant, unimportant people. *Everything* depends on you. Your nation depends on you; your political leaders depend on you; the course of history depends on you. It is high time you realized this.

An additional picture of activity in the spiritual realm is provided for us in the twenty-fourth chapter of Isaiah. This passage depicts a final, tremendous, climactic judgment that will close this age. It is a time when the whole earth will reel to and fro, be turned upside down, and be shaken like a cottage or a hut in an earthquake. The coming of the Lord in glory is described as occurring at the close of this period. Isaiah 24:21 says, *"It shall come to pass in that day that the Lord will punish on high the host of exalted ones, and on the earth the kings of the earth."*

Here we see the two realms again: *"the kings of the earth"* and *"the host of exalted ones"* (in the heavenly realm) who are going to be punished by God. That is the way it is: behind the visible is the invisible; behind the natural is the spiritual. And what takes place in the spiritual realm is decisive.

When you have victory in the spiritual realm, you have victory—period. Everything that follows in the natural, social, historical plane is a result of what has been achieved in the spiritual realm. That is why the church is completely able to change the course of the natural and the historical. All that is needed is for us to secure the victory in the spiritual realm.

GOD GIVES US SPIRITUAL WEAPONS

To close this chapter, let me direct your attention to one last passage of Scripture. One of the aspects I love about the Bible is that it is perfectly logical. Since we are engaged in a spiritual conflict, what kind of weapons do we need? Spiritual weapons. And that is what we have been given:

> *For though we walk in the flesh, we do not war according to the flesh. For the weapons of our warfare are not carnal but mighty in God for pulling down strongholds, casting down arguments and every high thing that exalts itself against the knowledge of God, bringing every thought into captivity to the obedience of Christ.* (2 Corinthians 10:3–5)

We walk in the earthly realm, living in bodies of flesh in a world bound by time. But our warfare is not in that realm. Our warfare is in the spiritual realm. Appropriately, the weapons that God has given us correspond to the realm in which we have to fight. We cannot win with guns, tanks, or missiles, because they just do not reach the enemy we are dealing with.

Rulers in our present day are frustrated because they do not have the means to intervene where the outcomes are really decided. But you and I do have the means. The weapons of our warfare are not carnal but mighty in God for pulling down Satan's strongholds in the unseen realm.

Please notice the words in 2 Corinthians 10:5 that show how our weapons affect humanity: "*...casting down arguments [reasoning] and every high thing that exalts itself against the knowledge of God, bringing every thought into captivity to the obedience of Christ.*" Strongholds, arguments, knowledge, and thoughts are all in the unseen realm. It is that realm that controls a person's thinking, reasoning, and knowledge. The warfare of the church is in that realm, and God has given us spiritual weapons that will insure spiritual victory—if we use them.

You may be asking yourself, *How do I use these spiritual weapons?* This will be our theme in upcoming chapters: how to get the victory in the spiritual realm.

As we conclude part 1 of this book, I believe it is appropriate to invite you to pray about a specific theme: that God may equip you and enable you to play the part in the world that He is expecting you to play. Perhaps you feel that up until now, you have not really been playing that part. Maybe you haven't even been aware that God has called you to spiritual warfare. Yet now, having seen from His Word that you are called, you are a willing volunteer.

If that is the case, then I would suggest that you go to God's altar in this moment of truth and just tell Him of your willingness. Offer yourself to God as a volunteer for the spiritual conflict—particularly as a volunteer in the spiritual conflict that will settle the destiny of your nation.

Father in heaven, I offer myself to You as a volunteer for the spiritual conflict to which You have called me. I ask You to especially use me to do battle in the spiritual conflicts that are being waged over my nation in the heavenly place right now.

Please use me, like Daniel, to fulfill Your purposes on earth through prayer and spiritual warfare in the Spirit. Equip me to play the part in the world that You have prepared for me, as I rely fully on You and Your mighty power. In Jesus' name, amen.

PART II

CHRIST HAS WON THE VICTORY

CHAPTER 6

THE DEVIL'S MOST GUARDED SECRET

As we continue our focus on the vital role we play in the history of our nations, I believe you are about to read what is perhaps the most important message God has ever given to me for the church. Why do I say this? Because I plan to expose and unfold to you the one fact that the devil is more determined than anything else to keep from the knowledge of God's people. I will endeavor to devote all my energy and every ability God has given me to make this message plain to you.

Our theme has been that we—the church—are the salt of the earth, the light of the world, and a city that is set on a hill. We occupy a unique position in the world, with singular privileges and responsibilities. The course and destiny of the nations in which we live—all the nations of the world—depend on us. If we fail by not exercising the responsibility and not fulfilling the position God has given us according to His Word, then we are salt that has lost its flavor. As Jesus said in the Sermon on the Mount, we are then *"good for nothing but to be thrown out and trampled underfoot by men"* (Matthew 5:13).

Let's look once again at these words in Matthew 5, reading them in the form I previously presented to you in which we changed *"you"* to "we," and *"it is"* to "we are." Reading them in this way heightens their application to us personally.

We are the salt of the earth; but if the salt loses its flavor, how shall it be seasoned? We are then good for nothing but to be thrown out and trampled underfoot by men.

I want to reemphasize a major reason why we occupy this unique position of responsibility: It is because we are engaged in a spiritual conflict with unseen—but absolutely real—spiritual forces and personalities that dominate the unregenerate world in which we live. We are *the only agency on earth* that has the power and ability to intervene in the spiritual realm. Therefore, as I said earlier, when we change the condition of the spiritual realm by using the spiritual weapons God has given us, we change the course of events here on earth. We alone are responsible for doing this.

CHRIST HAS ALREADY WON THE VICTORY

I will now highlight the basis of all spiritual victory. In due course, I am going to concentrate on the different spiritual weapons God has given us. But the exercise of these weapons depends on a clear and proper understanding of one great biblical fact. If we do not understand this fact, we cannot adequately or effectively use any of these spiritual weapons of warfare.

This great scriptural fact, which is clearly revealed in the New Testament, is very simply this: *Christ has already totally defeated all the enemies against whom we are contending.*

This is a great historical fact. It is not something that *is going* to happen; it is something that *has already* happened.

To strengthen our grasp of this tremendous truth, let us first look at the opening chapter of the apostle Paul's epistle to the Colossians:

For by Him [Jesus] all things were created that are in heaven and that are on earth, visible and invisible, whether thrones or dominions or principalities or powers. All things were created through Him and for Him.
(Colossians 1:16)

Please notice that in speaking about "all created things," Paul divided them into two realms—the heavenly and the earthly; the invisible and the visible.

I would like to draw your attention to the fact that Paul did not record any specific visible, earthly items in the above verse. But he described in detail the four main orders in the invisible spiritual realm, listing them according to their preeminence: *"thrones," "dominions," "principalities,"* and *"powers."* In the unseen spiritual realm, the *"thrones"* are the highest level—this was the realm John was caught up to, as depicted in Revelation 4 and 5. Note that one of the key words in Revelation 4:2–4 is *"throne"*:

> *Immediately I was in the Spirit; and behold, a throne set in heaven, and One sat on the throne. And He who sat there was like a jasper and a sardius stone in appearance; and there was a rainbow around the throne, in appearance like an emerald. Around the throne were twenty-four thrones, and on the thrones I saw twenty-four elders sitting, clothed in white robes; and they had crowns of gold on their heads.*

The King James Version reads, *"And round about the throne were four and twenty **seats**: and upon the seats I saw four and twenty elders sitting"* (Revelation 4:4). But the correct translation for *"seats"* is *"thrones."* Not only was God on His throne, but the twenty-four elders around Him were also on thrones. The thrones level is the highest level in the universe.

The level just below thrones encompasses *"dominions,"* or, more literally, "lordships." Then we come to *"principalities,"* or "rulerships"; and very closely associated with rulerships are always *"powers,"* or, more correctly, "authorities." Here we have revealed by Scripture what we could never know by natural reasoning—the four main orders of the unseen spiritual realm: thrones, lordships, rulerships, and authorities.

A DEFEATED REBEL EMPIRE

As we have noted, the Bible also reveals very clearly that sin and rebellion against God did not begin on the earthly realm but in the heavenly realm. The leader of all rebellion against God was and is a fallen angel whose name became Satan. People sometimes ask, "Why did God create Satan?" The answer is that God did not create Satan. God created a wonderful, glorious, angelic being named Lucifer. But when Lucifer rebelled, he became Satan. In Hebrew, the name *Satan* literally means "the adversary, the resister, the enemy." And that is what he is.

> CHRIST HAS TOTALLY DEFEATED ALL THE ENEMIES AGAINST WHOM WE ARE CONTENDING.

There is no record in Scripture of rebellion on the thrones level or the dominions level. The highest level on which there was rebellion against God was the level of principalities, or rulerships. That was where Satan was located. It is possible that he was the greatest, most powerful, most preeminent of all the princes, or principalities. But we do not know this for certain.

From the time of Satan's rebellion, there has been a certain sector within the realm of principalities (rulerships) and powers (authorities) that has been in opposition to almighty God, setting up a rebel empire opposed to Him and His kingdom. This empire is still in existence today. Subsequently, Satan involved the Adamic race in the same rebellion against God of which he himself had first been guilty in heaven. When Jesus Christ came to earth, one of the great things He accomplished by His death and resurrection was to finally terminate the authority of Satan. Christ defeated principalities and powers.

Very few Christians adequately grasp this fact. Christ has *already* defeated the principalities and powers that were arrayed against God and man.

THREE ACCOMPLISHMENTS OF THE CROSS

Jesus' absolute victory over the rulers of darkness is clearly stated in the second chapter of Colossians. The following passage tells us of three triumphs Jesus won by His death on the cross:

And you, being dead in your trespasses and the uncircumcision of your flesh,
He has made alive together with Him, having forgiven you all trespasses,
having wiped out the handwriting of requirements that was against us, which
was contrary to us. And He has taken it out of the way, having nailed it to
the cross. Having disarmed principalities and powers, He made a public
spectacle of them, triumphing over them in it.   (Colossians 2:13–15)

Let us examine the three great facts—each one of them essential—
that were achieved by the death of Jesus Christ.

1. WE WERE FORGIVEN

The first great fact is that we were forgiven of all our trespasses. (See
Colossians 2:13.) Through the death of Jesus Christ, it has become possible for God to justly forgive all our trespasses, because the just punishment of our trespasses has already been borne by Jesus Christ in our
place.

2. THE LAW AS A REQUIREMENT WAS ABOLISHED

The second great fact is that Jesus wiped out the handwriting of
requirements that was against us. (See Colossians 2:14.) The book of
Ephesians speaks of the same truth:

Having abolished in His flesh the enmity, that is, the law of command-
ments contained in ordinances....   (Ephesians 2:15)

These verses in Colossians and Ephesians run closely parallel, rein-
forcing for us that the second great achievement of the death of Jesus
Christ was to put an end to the law. *"For Christ is the end of the law for*
righteousness to everyone who believes" (Romans 10:4). The role of the law
as a means to righteousness acceptable to God ceased when Jesus died
on the cross. No one can now—or ever—commend himself to God by
the keeping of the law in any point whatsoever.

The following verses affirm this truth: *"Therefore, my brethren, you*
also have become dead to the law through the body of Christ" (Romans 7:4).
"For sin shall not have dominion over you, for you are not under the law but

under grace" (Romans 6:14). *"Knowing this: that the law is not made for a righteous person"* (1 Timothy 1:9).

When you are made righteous by faith in Jesus Christ, the law is not made for you. This truth is tremendously important. Multitudes of Christians are still half-entangled with the yoke of bondage to the law.

3. PRINCIPALITIES AND POWERS WERE DISARMED

The third great accomplishment of the cross is this: *"Having disarmed ["spoiled" KJV] principalities and powers, He [Jesus] made a public spectacle of them, triumphing over them in it"* (Colossians 2:15). When Jesus *"disarmed,"* or *"spoiled,"* His enemies, He stripped them of all their armor and weapons. Having done so, He triumphed over them. He put them to *an open, manifest, total, irremediable defeat.* This has already happened. It is not *going to* happen; it *has* happened.

In Luke's gospel, Jesus gave us a parable that illustrates His triumph:

> *When a strong man, fully armed, guards his own palace, his goods are in peace. But when a stronger than he comes upon him and overcomes him, he takes from him all his armor in which he trusted, and divides his spoils.* (Luke 11:21–22)

The fully armed strong man guarding his own palace is Satan. The *"stronger than he"* that came upon him is Jesus.

Notice the two acts that Jesus performed when He came upon Satan. First, He took from him *"all his armor in which he trusted."* We read in Colossians 2:15 that Jesus *"disarmed"* Satan. So, first, He stripped him of all his armor. Second, He spoiled his goods. Jesus delivered Satan's captives—He took away those whom the enemy had been in control of. Jesus made it possible for men and women who had been captives of Satan—his goods, his chattels—to be gloriously set free.

I cannot stress how important these three facts are for you. You must know and understand the impact of the crucifixion of Jesus—the victories that were accomplished by His death on the cross. Let me restate them:

First, the cross made it possible for God to forgive us of all our trespasses.

Second, the law was finally ended as a means for righteousness, and it will never be accepted as such again.

Third, Jesus totally defeated the principalities and powers that were arrayed in rebellion against God and man. He made an open show of them and spoiled them of all their weapons. This is the most tremendous fact.

WHEN JESUS "DISARMED" HIS ENEMIES, HE STRIPPED THEM OF ALL THEIR ARMOR AND WEAPONS.

If only Christians could fully realize that Satan does not even have any armor. Not only has he been defeated, but his armor has also been taken from him. Again, the majority of Christians creep around as though Satan had all the weapons, and, if they are lucky, maybe they can manage to hold him off somehow. Oh, how clever the enemy has been! But Satan has only one weapon left. Do you know what it is? Bluff! That is his only weapon—but he is a master at using it.

WE WERE CREATED TO HAVE DOMINION

This most tremendous fact—that Jesus totally defeated Satan and stripped him of his weapons—is the central theme of the Bible. It is crucial for the church to grasp this truth and to understand its scriptural basis. To do this, we must go back to the origin of the Adamic race, the race of Adam and his descendants. In Genesis 1:26, we find this record of the creation of Adam:

> *Then God said, "Let Us make man in Our image, according to Our likeness; let them have dominion over the fish of the sea, over the birds of the air, and over the cattle, over all the earth and over every creeping thing that creeps on the earth."*

Notice certain fundamental facts. First of all, God made man in His own likeness and in His own image. *"Likeness"* refers to the inner man;

"*image*" refers to the outer man. Adam was made like God in his moral and spiritual makeup, unlike any other lower created being. But he was also made like God in his actual outward appearance. Throughout Scripture, the word "*image*" consistently means "the outward form." Man looked like God. To some people, this might be a shocking statement, but it is the truth.

Let me explain it to you in this way: It was appropriate that when God came to earth in the Person of Jesus, He should be manifested in the form of a man—not as an ox or as a beetle. It was the human form that was fitting for the manifestation of the Son of God when He came in the flesh. So then, when Adam was created, he resembled God in outward appearance.

Second, notice that it was not merely Adam but the whole race that was involved in God's purposes. Genesis 1:26 says, "*Let them...*"—not "Let *him....*" "**Let them** have dominion."

The third great fact is that Adam was created (along with all of his race) to have dominion, or lordship, over all creation. It is important to understand that everything that was lost in the first Adam was restored in the last Adam, who is Jesus Christ. (See 1 Corinthians 15:45–49.) That includes dominion. Unfortunately, the great majority of Christians have absolutely no concept of this truth, partly because they do not realize what the first Adam was like.

The first Adam was a wonderful being. He outwardly resembled God, and he was intended to exercise authority on God's behalf over the entire domain in which God had set him.

And notice his domain! It was not a little patch of ground. It was "*over all the earth.*" He was created to exercise dominion as God's representative, visibly showing forth God's appearance over all the earth. Adam's dominion included "*the birds of the air.*" This point is important because it means Adam's dominion extended up from the surface of the earth into the lower air.

So here was Adam, showing forth God's likeness, and placed in this situation, authorized to exercise God's rule over the earth on His behalf. But what happened? In very simple language, he sold out to God's great rival. The devil came along and incited Adam and his wife to commit the same rebellion against God that he himself had previously committed in heaven. We see this fact in the words of temptation Satan used in Genesis 3:5:

> *For God knows that in the day you eat of it your eyes will be opened, and you will be like God, knowing good and evil.*

Earlier, I pointed out that a major component of Satan's fall was his last aspiration: *"I will be like the Most High"* (Isaiah 14:14). It is significant that when he tempted Adam and Eve, he ended his temptation with this same thought: *"'You will be like God.'* You won't need God; you will be like God yourselves. You won't need to depend on God, you won't need to seek His counsel and advice, and you won't need to obey Him. You can do the whole thing yourself just as well, without Him. Listen to me, and you won't have to bother about listening to God any longer." Haven't all of us been tempted by those thoughts?

THE SCOPE OF ADAM'S FALL

This is a vital truth: When Adam fell, he did not fall merely as an individual. His fall caused him not only to deliberately sell himself out, but also to sell out the entire domain given to him by God's authority. He sold out everything into the hand of God's great enemy, the devil. That is why the fall of Adam produced such a cataclysmic effect on the whole of creation. That is why thorns and thistles came up. That is why animals no longer lived in harmony and peace. When Adam fell, all of the realm of his dominion was ceded to Satan—a fact that the devil knew very well would be the case.

Read what the devil said to Jesus when he appeared to Him in the temptation in the wilderness:

> *Then the devil, taking Him up on a high mountain, showed Him all the kingdoms of the world in a moment of time. And the devil said to Him, "All this authority I will give You, and their glory; **for this has been delivered to me**, and I give it to whomever I wish."* (Luke 4:5–6)

The Greek word translated as *"delivered"* is correctly rendered as "betrayed." The same word is used of Judas betraying Jesus. So, when Adam fell, not only did he sell himself to the devil, but he also betrayed his entire God-given dominion into the hands of the enemy. Adam had legally been master of that entire dominion. Therefore, by handing it over to Satan, he made Satan the legal master of the dominion.

ADAM WAS CREATED
(ALONG WITH
ALL OF HIS RACE)
TO HAVE DOMINION,
OR LORDSHIP,
OVER ALL CREATION.

This truth is acknowledged in Scripture by the Lord Jesus Himself. As we discussed earlier, in three passages, Jesus called Satan *"the prince ["ruler"* NKJV] *of this world"*—and so he is. (See John 12:31 KJV; 14:30 KJV; 16:11 KJV.) How did Satan become the prince, or ruler? By persuading the one who was the ruler—the one who had the dominion—to turn himself and his dominion over to him. Since Satan had usurped the dominion that originally had been committed to Adam, he said to Jesus, in effect, "All this was betrayed to me, and I'll offer it back to You if You will do one thing—just worship me." As we know, Jesus would not do that.

Recall that Paul also used the title of *"prince"* in reference to Satan:

And you He made alive, who were dead in trespasses and sins, in which you once walked according to the course of this world, according to the prince of the power [the realm of authority] ***of the air,*** *the spirit who now works in the sons of disobedience....* (Ephesians 2:1–2)

In Greek, two words are used to express the concept of "air": *aer* and *aither*. These words give us the two English words *air* and *ether*. The word *aer*, which is used in this verse, means the air nearest to the surface of the earth.

Adam had dominion over the birds of the air, including the region in which they flew. So, when Adam fell, the entire area over which he had control, including the region immediately contiguous to the earth's surface—all the way around it—was handed over to Satan. As a result, according to Scripture, the devil became the prince, or ruler, of this area of authority, the literal translation of which is *"of the air."*

It is necessary for us to understand this reality and how it came about. Therefore, in the next chapter, we will examine these truths even more closely, with the help of a simple parable.

CHAPTER 7

RESTORING THE FAMILY BUSINESS

In chapter 6, we learned that God had originally entrusted to Adam the dominion of the whole earth. But when Adam fell, he deliberately sold himself, humankind, and his entire domain into the hand of God's archenemy, the devil. We traced how Adam's betrayal has been cataclysmic for all creation. With the authority that once belonged to Adam, Satan is now the ruler and prince of the power of the air. And in the unseen realm of principalities and powers, he has built a rebel empire that stands ready to do his bidding, bringing chaos, misery, and destruction to the entire world.

For our ultimate victory in spiritual warfare, it is crucial for us to understand this entire process and what Jesus did to buy back the domain that Adam lost. It will help each of us to fully come into our real position, privilege, and responsibility in the world. To help us grasp this truth, I want to illustrate it with a simple, imaginary story. It is my fervent hope that the following illustration will clearly communicate this process to you as you read it.

THE PARABLE OF THE WEALTHY BUSINESSMAN

Let's imagine a very wealthy man who is the founder and president of many businesses, one of which is running perfectly, making a wonderful profit every year. He decides to hand this business over to his son, whom he dearly loves. So, he puts the son in complete control of the company and says, "There you are. You run this business for me."

But this wealthy man has an unscrupulous, wicked rival who cheated and stole from him, and who absconded from his service years earlier. That person has set up a rival business organization. One day, this business rival—this crook and cheat—goes to the man's son and says, "You know, I don't know why you waste your time following your dad and doing what he tells you. That old man is out-of-date. He lives from a different age. People don't do things that way now. If you would just listen to me for a little while, I would show you how to be really smart in business. Why don't you let me take over the company? I will make you the executive vice president, and things will really move! Just listen to me and forget about your dad and all his old-fashioned ideas."

So, the young man foolishly hands over himself and his business to the control of this crook. Of course, the old man's secretary tells the father, "Do you know what has happened? Your son has handed over to your rival both himself and all aspects of the business that you gave him and of which you appointed him to be the manager. What are you going to do? Are you going to file a lawsuit?"

The old man says, "Oh, no."

"You're not going to take action?"

"Oh, no."

"You mean to say, you're going to let that crook get away with it?"

"For the time being...yes."

"Why?"

"Well, I could take that old crook to court, but if I did that, I would have to take my son to court, too. So, for my son's sake, I'll wait and handle this situation another way."

The secretary then asks him, "What *are* you going to do?"

"Well, I'll tell you. I'm going to pay the price that is necessary to buy back the business. Even though it's still mine, and I could *legally* get it back, I'm going to buy the business at tremendous cost."

"Well," the secretary says, "I think that's really carrying philanthropy too far. And what are you going to do with the business when you've bought it back?"

"I'm going to put my son back in charge."

HOW GOD REDEEMED HUMANITY

Do you understand the parable? Is it clear to you?

God is the father. He put His son, Adam, in charge of the whole realm of earth (the family business). Adam sold out to the rival, Satan. At any time, God could have gotten back complete control of everything, justifiably, because all of creation is still legally His. He could have dealt with Satan at any moment.

Do you see? Because God is perfectly just, if He had followed the law in order to deal with Satan, He would have had to deal with Adam, too. But for the sake of Adam and his race, and with infinite longsuffering, He waited. Century after century, He waited until it was the right time to come to earth in the Person of the Lord Jesus Christ. Jesus paid the immeasurable price of His lifeblood to "buy back the business," fully redeeming humanity from sin and death and restoring human beings to their position in Him. God bought back humanity at the highest price ever bid in the universe—the blood of the only begotten Son of God.

Friend, this is the incredible news: Do you know what God wants to do? He wants to put you and me back in charge. If that isn't grace, I don't know what is! Because, you see, He is *the God of all grace*" (1 Peter 5:10).

How powerful it is for us to understand that century after century, God has tolerated Satan as the devil has walked up and down across this earth, even appearing in the presence of God! Can you fathom it? In the first chapter of the book of Job, when the *"sons of God"* came to appear in the presence of God, who came among them? Satan. (See Job 1:6.)

As far as I am able to understand, the angels did not identify him. It was only the Lord who said, in effect, "I see you, Satan. Where have you come from?" And Satan answered, "I have been walking up and down on the earth, going to and fro." (See Job 1:7.)

Think of the infinite forbearance of God. Allowing that braggart, that crook, that scoundrel to walk up and down, century after century, across the beautiful earth He created and still legally owns. Do you know what Satan was busy doing when the *"sons of God"* appeared before the Lord? He was accusing God's servant Job—telling nasty stories and making filthy insinuations about him, the most righteous man in the world. (See Job 1:7–11.)

This is exactly what Satan is busy doing today. Precisely the same activity. He is still going to and fro. He is still the "accuser of the brethren," accusing us day and night before the throne of God. (See Revelation 12:10.) Yet God tolerates him with infinite patience. Why? Because, first of all, the "family business" had to be bought back by the death of Jesus Christ.

POWER OVER THE ENEMY

When Christ bought back the business, He settled every legal claim against the Adamic race. Therefore, it is now possible for God, with perfect justice, to forgive the repentant sinner without compromising His justice.

OUR AUTHORITY IN JESUS INCLUDES DESTROYING THE POWER OF THE ENEMY IN THE WORLD AND FREEING HIS CAPTIVES.

But God still tolerates Satan. Do you know why? Because He wants to see you and me back in charge of the family business—and our authority in Jesus includes destroying the power of the enemy in the world and freeing his captives. First John 3:8 says, *"For this purpose the Son of God was manifested, that He might destroy the works of the devil."* And Jesus told His followers in Luke 10:19, *"Behold, I give you the authority to trample on serpents and scorpions, and over all the power of the enemy...."*

Rather than merely giving mental assent to the great truth we have just explored, let's seal it in our experience with a prayer. If you desire to respond to this wonderful truth, please pray the following:

> Father in heaven, I marvel at Your infinite grace in Your dealings with Your "family business." I am amazed that You are willing to put us back in charge, but I am so grateful for that fact.
>
> I accept Your offer! I say to You, Lord, that I am grateful and willing to receive back all that You originally gave to Adam, which had been usurped by the enemy. I receive it now with thanks. Amen.

CHAPTER 8

BACK IN CHARGE

I hope that the simple parable of the wealthy businessman illustrated for you what I believe to be one of the most vital facts for Christians today: that Jesus Christ paid the ultimate price for us through His death and resurrection and that He bought back the entire dominion that Adam had betrayed into Satan's hands.

In His wondrous grace, God wants to put us back in charge of all that was lost in Adam. I hope you voiced the prayer at the end of the previous chapter, receiving the "family business" that the Father has given us.

Now we will examine some key Scriptures and work out the application of this essential truth for our lives.

SON OF MAN, SON OF ADAM

In 1 Corinthians 15, Christ is called by two names: *"the last Adam"* and *"the second Man"*:

> *And so it is written, "The first man Adam became a living being." The last Adam became a life-giving spirit....The first man was of the earth, made of dust; the second Man is the Lord from heaven.*
> (1 Corinthians 15:45, 47)

Jesus Christ is *"the last Adam"*—the end of one Adamic order. He is also *"the second Man"*—the new Man and the Head of a new race. He is both. When Jesus came to earth, He came as the representative of the entire Adamic race. He was made Man. Of all the titles that Jesus used of Himself in the Gospels, He used one of them eighty times, which is about ten times more than any other. That title was *"Son of Man,"* or "Son of Adam," since the name *Adam* means "man." So, of all the titles He loved, the one He used the most was "Son of Adam," indicating, "I am the Son of Adam. I am the Representative of the entire Adamic race."

Everything Jesus did on the cross, He did as our personal Representative. He went to the cross to represent the race. He took upon Himself the guilt, the shame, the condemnation, the sin, the sickness, the pain, and the suffering of an entire race.

> *And the LORD has laid on Him the iniquity of us all.* (Isaiah 53:6)

> *And He Himself is the propitiation for our sins, and not for ours only but also for the whole world.* (1 John 2:2)

Whatever Jesus suffered on the cross was not on His own behalf. He suffered as our personal Representative.

> *For He made Him who knew no sin to be sin for us, that we might become the righteousness of God in Him.* (2 Corinthians 5:21)

Jesus was the final Representative of the Adamic race. All our guilt and all our shame was rolled up in one burden and laid on the last Adam, the great Burden-Bearer, the One who took it all on Himself. It was settled by the One who could say, *"'It is finished!'* There is nothing more to do." (See John 19:30.)

A NEW ORDER

On the third day, Jesus rose from the grave. When He arose, He was the Head of an altogether new order. He was the First Begotten from the dead, the Prince of the kings of the earth. These two descriptions of Him are always combined in the Scriptures. Let's look at this in Colossians 1:18:

> *And He is the head of the body, the church, who is the beginning* [the Beginning of a new order], *the firstborn* [First Begotten] *from the dead, that in all things He may have the preeminence* [the first place].

In the first creation, it was by Him or through Him that all things were created. (See John 1:3; Colossians 1:16.) He was before all things, and by Him all things exist. (See Colossians 1:17.) But in the new creation, Jesus is the Head, the Beginning, the First Begotten from the dead, the first who rose from the dead. John wrote in Revelation 1:5:

> *...and from Jesus Christ, the faithful witness, the firstborn from the dead, and the ruler over* ["prince of" KJV] *the kings of the earth.*
> (Revelation 1:5 KJV)

Because Jesus is the *"firstborn from the dead,"* He has become the *"prince of the kings of the earth."* Notice that the title *"prince,"* or *"ruler,"* is now attached to Him. Once, the prince of this world was Satan. But ever since our Lord's death and resurrection, Jesus has been the Prince of the kings of the earth.

I would like you to see all of this very clearly from the Scriptures. As a student of the Old Testament and as a minister to the Jews, it always delights me to look at messianic passages, which find their fulfillment in Jesus the Messiah. Let's look first at Psalm 89.

> *He shall cry to Me, "You are my Father, My God, and the rock of my salvation."* [This is Christ, crying out to the Father. Notice what the Father answers:] *Also I will make him My firstborn, the highest of* ["higher than" KJV] *the kings of the earth.*   (Psalm 89:26–27)

The above passage does not refer to pre-creation, where Jesus was the *Only Begotten* of the Father. Here, He is made the Firstborn by being *begotten again* from the dead. Can you see this truth? This is the new creation, the new order, of which Jesus is the Head and the Beginning.

Next, let's examine Psalm 2:

Why do the nations rage, and the people plot a vain thing? The kings of the earth set themselves, and the rulers take counsel together, against the LORD and against His Anointed. (Psalm 2:1–2)

According to the book of Acts, we know that the words of these verses were fulfilled when Jesus was tried before the Gentile ruler and before the Jewish court, and was condemned by both, being rejected and put aside. (See Acts 4:24–28.) At that time these *"rulers"* essentially said,

Let us break Their bonds [the bonds of the Triune God] *in pieces and cast away Their cords from us.* (Psalm 2:3)

In other words, the people said, "We won't have this Man to rule over us. We don't want this Jesus. *'We have no king but Caesar!'* (John 19:15)." I cannot but point out that this was the most disastrous statement the Jewish race ever made. *"We have no king but Caesar!"* Look at what they have suffered from "Caesar" ever since. But they chose it—they made the decision.

IDENTIFIED WITH HIM

Next, as we continue in Psalm 2, notice the reaction of almighty God:

He who sits in the heavens shall laugh; the LORD shall hold them in derision. Then He shall speak to them in His wrath, and distress them in His deep displeasure [This is what God says]: *"Yet I have set My King on My holy hill of Zion."* [In other words, "I have raised My Son up."] Then the Son replies in answer to the Father:] *"I will declare the decree: the LORD has said to Me, 'You are My Son, today I have begotten You.'"* (Psalm 2:4–7)

Once again, this passage is not referring to creation. It is referring to the resurrection. On that day, God "begat" Jesus again from the dead to be the Firstborn, the Head of a new race. We can prepare to praise the Lord, because it gets better and better. When we read 1 Peter, we realize that we are not left out of membership in this new race:

Blessed be the God and Father of our Lord Jesus Christ, who according to His abundant mercy has begotten us again to a living hope through the resurrection of Jesus Christ from the dead.... (1 Peter 1:3)

This verse means that not only did God the Father "beget" Jesus again, but, in Jesus, He also begat *us* again *"to a living hope through the resurrection of Jesus Christ from the dead."* This is the great transaction: Jesus, the Savior, identified Himself in all points with the sinner, so that the saved believer might in turn be identified in all points with the righteousness of the law. Do you understand this? Jesus identified Himself with us in our sin so that we might be identified with Him in His righteousness, victory, and triumph—that is the other half of the exchange. One half is complete. Jesus has completed it. The other half remains for you and me to make complete.

THE THREE "TOGETHERS"

To bring the picture full circle, let's examine Ephesians 2:5–6:

...even when we were dead in trespasses, [God] made us alive together with Christ (by grace you have been saved), and raised us up together, and made us sit together in the heavenly places in Christ Jesus....

Notice the three "togethers." Because of what Jesus has done on our behalf through faith, we are now so identified with Him in the sight of God that God has made us alive *"together,"* raised us up out of the tomb *"together,"* and made us sit in the heavenly places *"together."* Can you see how complete the identification is? Because Jesus identified Himself with sinners, the believer is now entitled to be identified with Jesus in all that followed: His death, His burial, His resurrection, and His ascension.

I love to show people that Christ's death and resurrection are recorded in the Old Testament. The New Testament clearly states that Christ *"was buried, and that He rose again the third day according to the Scriptures"* (1 Corinthians 15:4). But do you know which Old Testament Scripture said that Jesus would rise from the dead on the third day? I know of only one:

Come, and let us return to the LORD; for He has torn, but He will heal us; He has stricken, but He will bind us up. After two days He will revive us; on the third day He will raise us up, that we may live in His sight.

(Hosea 6:1–2)

The wonderful thing is that this Scripture does not say that Jesus alone was raised up on the third day. It says that we were raised up *with Him.* Can you see that? God did not intend to bring only Jesus out of the dead *but a whole new race* as well. Every person who has put his or her faith in Jesus Christ is *"begotten…again to a living hope through the resurrection of Jesus Christ from the dead"* (1 Peter 1:3). It is as sure as if you saw me go underwater and then come up headfirst. The moment you saw my head appear, you would expect, by natural law, that the rest of my body would be sure to follow as I emerged from the water. Since Jesus, the Head, rose from the dead, it is just as certain that, by spiritual law, the rest of His body must follow.

GOD HAS GIVEN US AUTHORITY

The above, in itself, is wonderful news for us. But I have saved the best news for now. What did Jesus do next? Having done everything we have just reviewed—having settled every claim against the human race, having initiated a new race and made it possible for the devil to be totally silenced, having totally defeated the enemy—do you know what Jesus did? He did just what the father did in the little parable I told you. He said to us, "Here you are. Take back the business and run it for Me. I'm going back to heaven. It's now your job to see that things go right." It is a remarkable fact, but absolutely true.

You see, the first Adam was God's visible representative, intended to exercise God's authority on His behalf. God never scrapped that plan. The devil hindered it, but he did not prevent it, because the plan was restored in the last Adam. We, as believers in Jesus Christ, are also God's visible representatives, going forth to exercise His authority on His behalf. Just as much as Adam was in charge of the first creation, we, with Christ's authority, are to exercise dominion over the world as it is today.

EXERCISING HIS AUTHORITY

Let me direct you now to two Scripture passages that will tell you this plainly: Matthew 28:18–19 and John 20:21. We will begin with the last chapter of the book of Matthew. After the resurrection, Jesus addressed His disciples, saying,

> *All authority has been given to Me in heaven and on earth.*
> (Matthew 28:18)

Satan had usurped the dominion over the earth that had been given to Adam. But Jesus bought it back. Can you comprehend that reality? Since the resurrection, Satan no longer has had legal authority. Any authority he takes now is usurped. He no longer has legal claim to it, because, on the cross, Jesus settled every debt on behalf of the first Adamic race. Then Jesus rose again to become the Prince of the kings of the earth, and all authority in heaven and on earth was legally committed to Him by God the Father. That is why Jesus said, "All authority has now been vested in Me." What did He say next?

> *"Go therefore…."*
> (Matthew 28:19)

Do you see what was really happening? Jesus was not saying, "I am going to do it." He was saying, "*You* go and do it. *You* go to the world and demonstrate My authority." That is what His statement *"Go therefore"* amounts to: "You are My visible representatives, exercising My authority on My behalf."

In John 20:21, we have the same thought, but stated even more specifically. When Jesus appeared to His disciples on Resurrection Sunday, He said,

> *Peace be unto you: as my Father hath sent me, even so send I you.*
> (John 20:21 KJV)

"Even so" means "exactly so." Not approximately but exactly. Jesus was affirming, "Just exactly as My Father sent Me into this world, so now I am sending you."

FOUR IMPLICATIONS FOR US

There are four implications of this statement by Jesus in John 20:21. First, when Jesus the Son came, He said, *"I have come…not to do My own will, but the will of Him who sent Me.'* This is the whole purpose for My being in the world—not to do what I want but to do what the Father wants." (See John 6:38.)

JESUS ROSE AGAIN TO BECOME THE PRINCE OF THE EARTH, AND ALL AUTHORITY IN HEAVEN AND ON EARTH WAS LEGALLY COMMITTED TO HIM BY GOD.

Second, He said, "The works that I do, *'the Father who dwells in Me does the works.'* I don't do them." (See John 14:10.)

Third, He said, "*'The words that I speak to you'* are the Father's who sent Me." (See John 14:10, 24.)

Fourth, He said, *"He who has seen Me has seen the Father"* (John 14:9).

Therefore, in relation to Jesus' statement *"As my Father hath sent me, even so send I you"* (John 20:21 KJV), we see that all four of these Scriptures bring out important truths for us.

Truth #1: We are here not to do our own will but to do the will of Jesus Christ who sent us. We have no right to be doing our own will. The only reason that we are here is to do Jesus' will.

Truth #2: Whatever we do, we should be able to say, "It is not I who am doing it. It is Christ in me doing the work."

Truth #3: Whatever words we speak, we should be able to say, "These are not my words. They are the words that Christ gave me."

Truth #4: We should be able to stand in front of this world and say, "If you have seen me, you have seen Christ." In fact, we cannot avoid this connection, because we are the visible representatives of the Godhead. Just as much as Adam was made in the likeness and image of God in order to exercise God's authority on His behalf, so we have been re-created in the image and likeness of God through Jesus Christ to exercise God's authority on His behalf. Jesus has gone back to heaven. Whatever has to be done now on earth must be done by you and me.

Let us close this chapter with Ephesians 3:10, which speaks of God's ultimate purpose in redemption:

To the intent that now the manifold wisdom of God might be made known by the church to the principalities and powers in the heavenly places....

In other words, we are to be the demonstration of the manifold wisdom of God—not merely to this world but also to the whole realm of principalities and powers in the heavenly places. The manifold, many-sided wisdom of God is to be unfolded, revealed, and perfected in the church—and that means you and me. That is why we are here. That is God's purpose.

Are you able to absorb the magnitude of this responsibility? Even more, are you prepared to accept it? If so, offer yourself to the Lord in prayer:

Lord, as incredible as it may seem to me, I recognize that as a Christian, I am Your visible representative in the earth. Please pour out Your enabling grace upon me. I offer myself in service to You and ask You to strengthen me to accurately and effectively represent You, Your righteousness, and Your authority in the world around me. This I will do, with Your help and grace. I am Yours, O Lord. Amen.

In the next chapter, we will further explore the use of each of the spiritual weapons placed at our disposal by the Lord. In addition, we will affirm the fact—first and foremost—that Satan has already been defeated. However, it is up to us to administer the victory Christ has already won, utilizing every weapon He has given us.

PART III

THE POWER OF PRAYER AND FASTING

CHAPTER 9

TAKING UP OUR WEAPONS

I have pointed out that the church has a unique position and responsibility as salt and light to the world. Let's once again read Matthew 5:13 in the form that places the responsibility upon ourselves. (I encourage you to declare this statement out loud, if possible.) Are you ready?

> We are the salt of the earth; but if the salt loses its flavor, how shall it be seasoned? We are then good for nothing but to be thrown out and trampled underfoot by men.

As the church of Jesus Christ, we are the decisive factor in human affairs. The destiny of men, nations, and civilizations depends upon us. The primary reason is that the destiny of men and nations is settled by spiritual forces in the unseen spiritual realm. The church alone is able to intervene in that realm.

With spiritual weapons, we can overcome those forces of evil, thus changing the influences and the powers that are at work upon humanity. In this way, we can bring about a positive transformation for the glory of God in the affairs of the human race. Particularly, I would point out that as Christians, no matter what nation we live in, we are accountable to God for the general condition of that nation—both political and spiritual.

PAGEANT OF TRIUMPH

What is the basis of our power and authority to intervene effectively in the spiritual realm? It is the fact that Jesus Christ, by His death and resurrection, put all the forces of evil to a final defeat and open shame. He did this as our Representative—the last Adam, the One who represented the entire Adamic race, taking upon Himself all our guilt, all our failure, all our condemnation, and every heavy burden that sin has brought on us. He met our enemy face-to-face, defeated him, and rose as our Representative and as the Head of a new race to lead us forth in victory and in triumph.

Paul described this truth for us in Colossians:

> *Having disarmed principalities and powers, He made a public spectacle of them, triumphing over them in it.*   (Colossians 2:15)

Jesus Christ has triumphed over principalities and powers, making an open show of them at the cross. The word *triumph* in this sense means "a public official celebration of a victory that has already been won." A triumph is not the same as a victory. The victory is the winning of the battle. The triumph is the celebration of the victory. Christ has triumphed openly over principalities and powers. He leads an open pageant of triumph as those enemies trail along in chains behind Him.

WE CAN BRING ABOUT A POSITIVE TRANSFORMATION FOR THE GLORY OF GOD IN THE AFFAIRS OF THE HUMAN RACE.

Paul's reference to a triumph was actually taken from the customs of ancient Rome. In the Roman Empire, when a general was outstandingly successful in a campaign, adding new territories or conquering great enemies, the senate at Rome officially voted him a "triumph."

He was placed in a chariot drawn by a white horse and was led in parade through the streets of the city. The citizens of Rome lined the streets, applauding him as he went past. Behind the general, the evidences of his conquests were led in chains.

For instance, if he had been to a land inhabited by tigers, some captured tigers would be led in pageant behind him as evidence of his victory (especially since this animal was not common in Rome). In addition, any kings or great military leaders whom he had defeated would be led in chains behind his chariot. Following them would be rank after rank of captives taken prisoner during the war. Again, the captured enemies that followed behind the general were the public evidences of the victories he had won.

Paul attributed this vivid picture to Jesus Christ. We envision Christ in the chariot, having defeated all our foes through the cross and now leading them in public subjection and submission behind Him. This is the picture that the word *triumph* would have conjured up for the believers in the days of the apostle Paul, and it should for us as well. It is the open, official, public celebration of a victory that has already been won. It is an exhibition of all the forces that have been defeated. By virtue of His sacrifice on the cross, Jesus has led Satan and all his principalities and powers behind Him in open defeat and subjugation.

Moving forward, we find a tremendous verse in 2 Corinthians:

Now thanks be to God who always leads us in triumph in Christ, and through us diffuses the fragrance of His knowledge in every place.
(2 Corinthians 2:14)

Christ has already triumphed, but this statement tells us that God always leads us to triumph in Christ. The end of the verse says *"in every place."* If we consider that the verse adds together *"always"* and *"in every place,"* that doesn't leave anything out, does it? We are *always* caused to triumph in Christ.

Please bear in mind that the picture here is not that we join the captives in chains behind His chariot. No, we belong *in* the chariot with Him. By right, that is the place of every believer. Jesus invites us to share His triumph. One of the new translations renders 2 Corinthians 2:14 as, *"Wherever I go, thank God, he makes my life a **constant pageant of triumph** in Christ..."* (MOFFATT).

A *"pageant of triumph"* is what we ought to be and what we have the right to be. We are the representatives of Jesus Christ. He won the victory. Now He has left it to you and me to apply the victory. As we saw earlier, Jesus Himself said this in Matthew 28:18–19, which I have paraphrased here: "All power is given to Me in heaven and on earth. Go therefore and demonstrate it. Show the world the power that I have won by My death and resurrection."

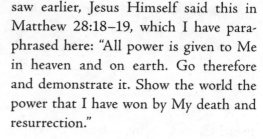

CHRIST WON THE VICTORY. NOW HE HAS LEFT IT TO YOU AND ME TO APPLY THE VICTORY.

Likewise, in John 20:21, Jesus said, *"As the Father has sent Me, I also send you."* Jesus was confirming that we are His visible representatives. We are in the world to demonstrate His victory, to apply His triumph, and to show the people of the world what He has achieved on their behalf.

OUR SPIRITUAL WEAPONS

With that as our foundation, we turn now to examine the weapons with which we do battle. Because we are in a spiritual war, it is only logical that God has provided us with spiritual weapons. In 2 Corinthians, we are told about these weapons:

> *For though we walk in the flesh, we do not war according to the flesh. For the weapons of our warfare are not carnal but mighty in God for pulling down strongholds, casting down arguments and every high thing that exalts itself against the knowledge of God, bringing every thought into captivity to the obedience of Christ....*
>
> (2 Corinthians 10:3–5)

Note that the opposing rebellious thoughts are also brought into captivity behind the chariot. That is where they belong. Just as we belong in the chariot, these rebels belong behind the chariot. All the rebel forces in the spirit realm that dominate men's minds, imaginations, and reasonings, causing them to revolt against God, are brought by us into captivity. As a result, they follow us in chains behind the chariot. To help us to understand this reality, Scripture emphasizes this truth: *"The weapons of our warfare are not carnal but mighty in God"* (2 Corinthians 10:4). To achieve the defeat of spiritual enemies, God has given us spiritual weapons.

At this point in our study, I am going to examine some of the primary spiritual weapons with which God expects us to attain these results. Briefly, I will enumerate what I believe to be the main weapons. However, I do not suggest for a moment that this list is exhaustive. Here are the ones we will discuss: prayer, fasting, praise, testimony, and preaching.

If we were to go on from these weapons, we would discuss the supernatural gifts of the Holy Spirit. (See, for example, 1 Corinthians 12:1–11.) However, for our purposes in this book, we will deal only with those I have listed above. In the chapters that lie ahead, I will focus on what I consider to be the spiritual weapons that primarily should concern the majority of God's people. We will begin with the weapon of prayer.

CHAPTER 10

THE GREAT POWERHOUSE

By way of introduction to the theme of prayer, I would like to focus on a passage in Matthew 18, spoken by Jesus:

> *Assuredly, I say to you, whatever you bind on earth will be bound in heaven, and whatever you loose on earth will be loosed in heaven. Again I say to you that if two of you agree on earth concerning anything that they ask, it will be done for them by My Father in heaven. For where two or three are gathered together in My name, I am there in the midst of them.* (Matthew 18:18–20)

THE POWER WE RECEIVE

The above passage is our great powerhouse as we encounter the world. In these verses are contained all the elements of power that we need to do anything we ever want to accomplish. No president, no dictator, no army commander, and no ordinary person outside the church has the smallest fraction of the power that is described and offered to all Christians in these verses.

"*Whatever you bind on earth will be bound in heaven, and whatever you loose on earth will be loosed in heaven…anything that they ask, it will be done for them*" (Matthew 18:18–19). What more could you ask than that? There is absolutely nothing—no situation, no problem, no enemy, no opposition—that is left outside of those promises. Everything you need to be totally effective and totally victorious is contained there.

In offering a few comments on this passage, I would like to give you the "Prince Version" of Matthew 18:20. This is my own literal translation: "For where two or three have been led together into My name, I am there in the midst."

You will notice that I have changed the phrase *"are gathered together"* to "have been led together." My basis for this change is found in Romans 8:14:

For as many as are led by the Spirit of God, these are sons of God.

We cannot leave out the Holy Spirit in any Christian activity. Where two or three people have been led together by the Holy Spirit, that is where important action starts to happen.

INTO HIS NAME

Next, instead of the phrase *"in My name,"* I prefer to translate it "into My name." This gives the correct impression that the name of the Lord Jesus Christ is the focal point around which His people meet. In actual fact, this is the only authorized meeting place for Christians in this dispensation. Under the Old Testament dispensation, when God brought Israel into the Promised Land, He said, in essence, "I will appoint one place where a house will be built. I will place My name there, and that is the only place in the land where I will accept your sacrifices and offerings." This place was Jerusalem, and the "house" was the temple that Solomon built. The important point to note is that God said, "You must not bring your sacrifices in any other place, for I have put My name in that house." (See Deuteronomy 12:11–14.)

WHERE TWO OR THREE PEOPLE HAVE BEEN LED TOGETHER BY THE HOLY SPIRIT, IMPORTANT ACTION STARTS TO HAPPEN.

The same standard is true in this dispensation. There is only one authorized basis of meeting together for Christians. We do not meet as Baptists or Presbyterians or Episcopalians. That is not what God has authorized. There is only one center into which we are entitled to come together, and that is into the name of Jesus. Where two or three have been led together into the name of Jesus by the Holy Spirit, Jesus promised, "I am there in your midst."

It is important to recognize that this eighteenth chapter of Matthew contains the second of only two statements in Jesus' discourses in the Gospels in which He spoke about the church. The first one is in Matthew 16:18, where Jesus said, *"On this rock I will build My church."* Here, in Matthew 18:17, Jesus taught:

> If he [an unrepentant believer] *refuses to hear them* [two or three other believers], *tell it to the church. But if he refuses even to hear the church, let him be to you like a heathen and a tax collector.*

I want to offer you my opinion on the two uses of the term *"church."* In Matthew 16, Jesus was talking about the universal church—the true body of all believers of all races, all ages, all backgrounds, and all denominations. That group of believers will not meet in one place until it meets in the rapture. (See 1 Thessalonians 4:15–17.) That will be the first time that the whole church will come together as the universal church. It is impossible to convene the universal church at this time on earth.

In Matthew 18, however, Jesus was speaking about the local church. Basically, His reference to the local church starts with verse 20. Let us read it again in the "Prince Version": "Where two or three have been led together into My name...." This is the basis of the true local church of Jesus Christ: two or three believers led together into the name of Jesus.

HEALTHY CELLS

Recognizing that the church is the body of Jesus Christ, we should all agree that it is important to care for the health of the church. I am not a medical doctor, but as I mentioned earlier, I served in the British Army as a medical orderly. So I have some knowledge concerning healthy bodies. Even speaking as a layman, the facts are so simple as to be self-evident: In the life of the physical body, a human being is the composite of a multiplicity of cells that comprise the entire body. When the cell life in someone's body begins to break down, that person starts to experience ill health. Nothing can substitute for the healthiness of the individual cells.

I would submit to you that exactly the same is true for the body of Jesus Christ. In Matthew 18, we see the "cell life" of the church: two or three believers who have been led together into the name of Jesus. If this cell life ceases to be healthy, no matter what else we may do on a larger scale—no matter what programs or revivals or conferences we may have—the body of Jesus Christ will basically remain unhealthy. Individual cell life is a must for healthy function. The body of Jesus Christ as a whole cannot function healthily—any more than your body can be healthy—when the individual cell life has been broken down.

As you know, cancer and various other diseases like it are essentially the result of the breaking down of the cell life in the body. Ultimately, if the breakdown continues, the entire body can be destroyed.

I am convinced that the same is true of the church. If the cell life of the "two or three"—the individual close fellowship of people brought together into the name of Jesus—is not healthy, then the body of the church as a whole cannot be healthy. In the next chapter, we will discuss how we can foster healthy cell life and thus prevent breakdown.

CHAPTER 11

RIGHT RELATIONSHIPS

In considering Matthew 18:18–20, we have already seen that this passage identifies the source of all spiritual power. All power that may ever be required for any need is contained in the promises of these verses. But I believe the Bible tells us that this powerhouse is surrounded by a great fence. You cannot get into this secret central area of power except through that fence. And that fence is right relationships. If you do not maintain and live in right relationships with other people, you cannot access the great powerhouse of prayer.

BE RIGHT WITH GOD AND MAN

Jesus instructed us on this vital element just a few verses prior to the above verses on prayer. In Matthew 18:15, He said, *"Moreover if your brother sins against you, go and tell him his fault between you and him alone."* Put it right. Don't neglect to deal with offenses and misunderstandings.

Then, at the close of Matthew 18, Jesus told the parable of the unforgiving servant who was forgiven a debt of ten thousand talents—yet he would not forgive the debt of a mere one hundred denarii that was owed to him. That servant was delivered to the torturers as a consequence. The last verse of that parable says:

So My heavenly Father also will do to you if each of you, from his heart, does not forgive his brother his trespasses. (Matthew 18:35)

Unforgiveness, resentment, wrong attitudes, and broken relationships exclude the Christian from the place of powerful prayer. Multitudes of Christians know nothing of the potency that is in that place of prayer because they do not maintain right relationships with other people. Please allow me to offer you an important blanket statement: You cannot be wrong with man and right with God. It is impossible. If you are right with man, you can be right with God. And if you are right with God, you will be right with man.

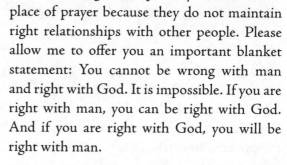

IF YOU ARE RIGHT WITH GOD, YOU WILL BE RIGHT WITH MAN.

Let me emphasize this point with a very simple illustration. The cross of Christ has two beams—the vertical and the horizontal. Both are needed to make the complete cross, which represents two relationships. The vertical is the relationship of man to God; the horizontal is the relationship of man to man. If the horizontal beam is out of position, you do not need someone to tell you that the vertical beam is also out of position. If you are wrong with your fellow man, you cannot be right with God.

Let us consider how this illustration applies to relationships in the Christian life. One of the greatest sources of problems—the greatest leakage of power in the church—is wrong relationships. The sacred secret area of all power is absolutely fenced in by God's demand for harmony and reconciliation, which He will not vary. You must maintain right relationships with everybody. If you do not, you have no right of access to this vital area of prayer.

IRRESISTIBLE HARMONY

The breakdown of the home is probably the greatest weakness of evangelical Christianity. The son of a leading fundamentalist pastor in a major city once said to me, "I know about forty fundamentalist ministers personally—and out of all of them, I don't know one really happy home."

That statement is shocking, but it reveals an important truth: You can be absolutely right in all your doctrines and totally wrong in all your relationships. Christianity is not primarily a religion of doctrine—it is a religion of relationships. This is what the Holy Spirit is presently emphasizing to us. Let's get in harmony—then we will be irresistible in prayer.

This principle of harmony is conveyed in Matthew 18:19: *"If two of you **agree** on earth concerning anything that they ask…."* It is significant that the Greek word translated *"agree"* is the same word from which the English word *symphony* is derived. In other words, "If two of you shall symphonize on earth…."

This concept has nothing to do with mere intellectual agreement. I think it is an absolute travesty to the symphonizing that Jesus was talking about when Christians say, "Let's agree," yet they are not in agreement—they are far from right relationships with one another. The word *symphony* indicates harmony, concord, the melding together of two spirits in unity. When that happens, anything you ask will be done. You are irresistible! Nothing can stand before you.

I am not a musician—far from it. But I know that to have a musical symphony, at least two elements are needed: one is a conductor, and the other is a score. You can have all the components of an orchestra, but if you don't have a conductor and a score, there will be no symphony.

This concept applies spiritually as well. To have true spiritual symphony, you must have the Conductor and the score. The Conductor is the Holy Spirit; the score is the will of God revealed by the Holy Spirit. When two Christians come to harmony on the revealed will of God through the Holy Spirit, whatever they ask will be done. There are no failures. It is guaranteed.

AGREEMENT BETWEEN HUSBAND AND WIFE

Let me pose a question here: Normally speaking, who would be the two people most naturally to agree together in prayer? If your answer is husband and wife, you would be correct. But how many husbands and wives really do agree together?

I was once speaking at a gathering of Christian brothers, and I asked, "How many husbands here find it easy to agree with their wives?" Only one man out of a rather large crowd sheepishly put his hand up halfway. The fact of the matter is that the natural man doesn't find it easy to agree with anybody. Agreement is almost impossible for the old, unregenerate, quarrelsome, self-assertive ego of man; it is almost impossible in the old realm. It is possible only in the new man and in the new realm of Jesus Christ. (See, for example, Colossians 3:8–11.)

WHEN THE HOME IS BROKEN DOWN, ALL HUMAN LIFE IS ULTIMATELY BROKEN DOWN.

I fully believe there is no greater need in the church today than the agreement of husband and wife, father and mother. In every age and dispensation, from Adam and Eve to the present, there has been one central unit in all of human life, and that is the home. This focal point does not vary, and it will be that way until the close of human history. It was that way under the law; it is the same under grace. It was that way with the patriarchs; it will be the same in the millennium. The central unit of all human life is the home. When the home is broken down, all human life is ultimately broken down. I do not believe there can be any disputing of that fact.

And there is no greater single problem in the world today than the breakdown of the home. I have traveled widely as a speaker, and I have been interviewed from time to time by people who would consult me and ask me what I thought about the problems of the nation in which I was speaking. I was usually careful to tell them that since I was not a citizen of their country, I was not sure it was my business to solve the problems of their nation. Then they would ask me about other social issues. I would never presume to be an expert, but I would feel free to offer an opinion. Most frequently, I would comment that the most serious issue in the world today is the breakdown of the home. Without question, it remains the greatest single emergency that confronts the church worldwide. And it begins in the breakdown between husband and wife.

The breakdown of the union between a married couple is the source of all subsequent family problems. For example, if a father and mother are not united, they will never control their children. Children always know when there is disharmony between their parents. This problem affects many other realms of life as well. No matter from what point of view we consider a problem, it often centers in this relationship.

HINDERED PRAYERS

The apostle Peter gave a remarkable confirmation of the above supposition when writing about the relationship between husbands and wives:

> *Husbands, likewise, dwell with them* [wives] *with understanding, giving honor to the wife, as to the weaker vessel, and as being heirs together of the grace of life, that your prayers may not be hindered.*
>
> (1 Peter 3:7)

Have you ever made the connection Peter pointed out by those last seven words? What he was pointing out is that disharmony between husband and wife will hinder their prayers. This is just one example of the overall principle. In order to receive answers to our prayers, we must "symphonize." We must be in harmony. We must be in concord. We must be in spiritual unity. When we reach that place of spiritual unity, everything we ask will be done.

Let me be frank here. I am a husband myself. I know it is never easy for two people to live in real spiritual harmony. It requires attention. Both must realize the value of it, and it is only through the work of the cross in each spouse's life that it will ever be achieved. But the rewards are the greatest. Believe me, it is worth the effort to arrive at that place of unity.

If husbands and wives who believe in Jesus Christ and have the baptism of the Holy Spirit cannot live in harmony, they have nothing worthwhile to export to the rest of the world. The world has enough friction, frustration, division, and disharmony already. If that is all you have to offer to other people, keep it to yourself. Don't export it. The test of whether what we have really works is whether or not it works in the home. If it doesn't work in your home, don't try to make it work anywhere else.

Let me quickly add that in a home where one of the partners is an unbeliever, this is a different matter. Also, of course, husbands and wives are not the only two who can come together in prayer. But they are the most obvious two. As we observed earlier, when a husband and wife are in harmony, their prayers are irresistible. When a husband and wife agree with one another and touch God simultaneously, what they ask for is settled. It will be done.

However, I know from experience that the devil is also familiar with the principle of harmony, and he will do everything he can to introduce a little seed of discord, a little frustration, or a little friction. A disagreement doesn't have to be big or important for it to hinder your prayers.

TURNING THE HEARTS

I want to close this chapter with a very personal application. My hope is not to simply leave you feeling enthusiastic, because enthusiasm has a habit of waning. I believe that I should press you to the point of a real, intimate, personal decision, and I am going to do that right now. I have said that the two people most naturally to agree in prayer are husband and wife. My firm conviction is that if married couples would do this, it would be the most important change for good that could take place in our world at the present time.

Many people do not realize that in some Bible versions, the last word of the Old Testament is *"curse."* Did you realize that? God's last word under the old covenant was a *curse.* Thank God for the New Testament; otherwise, we would have been left with a curse. The last two verses of the Old Testament say this:

> *Behold, I will send you Elijah the prophet before the coming of the great and dreadful day of the* Lord. *And he will turn the hearts of the fathers to the children, and the hearts of the children to their fathers, lest I come and strike the earth with a curse.*   (Malachi 4:5–6)

Do you see the greatest single problem that will vex the earth in the last days? It is the breakup of the home. What is needed to avert this curse? We must see the hearts of the fathers turned back to their children, and the hearts of the children turned back to their fathers. The only cure that can turn back the curse is the restoration of the home.

I have preached often about the need for fathers to be reconciled with their children. I have said publicly that men have reneged on their responsibilities as husbands, fathers, and church leaders. They have left them to the women. Shame on them! But God has shown me that the main focal point of reconciliation is between husband and wife. Then the children can be brought back.

WILL YOU RESPOND?

What I have just described is a general principle, and I know that there are individual cases in which it may not be applicable. However, I believe that restored unity in the Christian home is the heart, core, and center of spiritual renewal. I am therefore going to ask now that husbands and wives alike who are reading this book will, with the help of almighty God, dedicate themselves and their homes to become centers of effective, united prayer on behalf of their nation.

Will you make that commitment? If you, as a husband or as a wife, want to dedicate yourself in this way, I would ask you to stand to your feet as you read this. If you are not in a place where you can physically stand right now, please at least imagine yourself standing before an altar in commitment and dedication to the Lord. By standing in this way, either

THE ONLY CURE
THAT CAN TURN BACK
THE CURSE IS
THE RESTORATION
OF THE HOME.

literally or figuratively, you are making a decision—as God enables you, and subject to all your human weaknesses—to dedicate yourself from this hour forward to pray in a new, effective way for divine intervention in the leadership of your nation and in all the nations of the world.

Now I want to pray for you regarding the personal decision you are making at this moment.

God, in the name of the Lord Jesus Christ, I come to You on behalf of every person who has stood to his or her feet, who has made the decision that I have outlined from Your Word. In the precious name of Jesus, I pray for each one that, from now on, Your blessing will rest upon them in a new way.

Lord, by a deliberate choice of their will, they have identified themselves with Your purposes for the world and for the extension of Your kingdom. On this basis, I ask You, from now on, to bless them, to unite them with their spouses in a new way, and to give them a new vision, a new dedication, a new purpose.

Please bless the home they represent. Where there is heartache, tragedy, and division—and where some are scattered and apparently lost—Lord, I pray now in the name of Jesus for the restoration of this home and for the restoration of the homes of all the families in their nation. In Jesus' name, amen.

CHAPTER 12

PRAYER—FIRST OF ALL

I have described the power of prayer with regard to believers who are in right relationship to one another. I now want to discuss prayer with regard to the realm of spiritual warfare.

As we explore this topic, our text will be 1 Timothy 2:1–4:

Therefore I exhort first of all that supplications, prayers, intercessions, and giving of thanks be made for all men, for kings and all who are in authority, that we may lead a quiet and peaceable life in all godliness and reverence. For this is good and acceptable in the sight of God our Savior, who desires all men to be saved and to come to the knowledge of the truth.

The passage we have just read is a wonderful presentation of logical truth, each step developing out of the previous one. In Paul's epistles to Timothy, his focus was on some of the basic needs of the church. Where did he begin? What did he cite first as a basic need of the church?

Paul listed several activities related to this need—supplications, prayers, intercessions, and the giving of thanks—but if I were to sum them up in one general word, it would be *prayer*. "First of all," Paul said, "we need prayer."

PRAY FOR THOSE IN AUTHORITY

The next verse identifies the first people on God's recommended prayer list for the church. We should pray *"for kings and all who are in authority"* (1 Timothy 2:2). In many large congregations of the United States where I have spoken, I have asked this question: "How many of you have prayed today for the president of the United States?" Sadly, I have never had a positive answer from more than 20 percent of the people. Never. Usually, the response is approximately 2 percent of the audience. If the members of the body of Christ will not pray for those in authority in their respective nations, who will? I sincerely believe that the Word of God means exactly what it says. The first item on the normal Christian's prayer list every day should be those in authority.

A QUIET AND PEACEABLE LIFE

What are we to pray for next? *"That we may lead a quiet and peaceable life in all godliness and reverence"* (1 Timothy 2:2). This is the request we are to make. How would you express what is most needed for us to lead such a life? I would sum it up with these two words: *good government.* This verse is really a definition of what good government should ensure: *"That we may lead a quiet and peaceable life in all godliness and reverence."*

Please ask yourself this question about the nation in which you live: Are the people here leading quiet and peaceable lives in all godliness and reverence? If not, why not? I believe the answer is that Christians have not prayed.

The disintegration and destruction we see happening in so many nations around the world was very accurately described centuries ago in the Word of God. This was God's message through the prophet Isaiah to the people of Israel in that day:

> *Your country is desolate, your cities are burned with fire; strangers devour your land in your presence; and it is desolate, as overthrown by strangers.* (Isaiah 1:7)

That is a fairly accurate description of what is occurring in many of the nations of the world today, isn't it? The remarkable feature of this passage is that God had to send a prophet to His people to tell them what was happening right in front of their eyes. You would think that if the people's land was being devoured and their cities were being burned with fire, they would be conscious of what was going on. But God had to send a prophet to tell them.

Do you know why they could not see what was happening in front of their eyes? They were too busy with religious activities— exactly the same as many modern Christians are. They were so occupied with "church" that they could not see what was occurring.

ARE THE PEOPLE OF YOUR NATION LEADING QUIET AND PEACEABLE LIVES OF GODLINESS AND REVERENCE?

What God says in the following passage points to this conclusion:

> *"To what purpose is the multitude of your sacrifices to Me?" says the* Lord. *"I have had enough of burnt offerings of rams and the fat of fed cattle. I do not delight in the blood of bulls, or of lambs or goats. When you come to appear before Me, who has required this from your hand, to trample My courts? Bring no more futile sacrifices; incense is an abomination to Me. The New Moons, the Sabbaths, and the calling of assemblies; I cannot endure iniquity and the sacred meeting. Your New Moons and your appointed feasts My soul hates; they are a trouble to Me, I am weary of bearing them."* (Isaiah 1:11–14)

While the world was burning right outside their sanctuaries, the Jews were busy with their religion—their programs, their committees, their promotion schemes, their membership drives. The world and their nation were sinking to ruin right in front of them, and they could not grasp the fact.

As far as I am concerned, that is an accurate portrait of many nations in the world today. Really, it is a severe condemnation of the modern church as well. We are no better than the people in the temple in the days of Isaiah. Too many of us in too many of our nations are simply busy with a religion that has no vital contact with reality and does not solve people's problems.

WHY GOOD GOVERNMENT?

Let's return now to the apostle Paul's exhortation in 1 Timothy 2. He told us in verse 2 that we are to pray *"for kings and all who are in authority, that we may lead a quiet and peaceable life in all godliness and reverence."*

In verse 3, Paul went on to say, *"For **this** is good and acceptable in the sight of God our Savior."* What was Paul referring to when he wrote *"this"*? Good government. Please ask yourself this question: Which does God approve of—bad government or good government? Which is pleasing to Him? The answer is obvious: good government.

In 1 Timothy 2:4, Paul gave us the most practical reason why God approves good government: He *"desires all men to be saved and to come to the knowledge of the truth."* In other words, God wants all men to have an opportunity to hear the truth of the gospel under the most favorable circumstances, and, as a result of hearing it, to be saved.

Common sense tells us that good government is more conducive to the work of preaching the gospel and reaching men for Christ. That is not difficult to see. Where there is violence, lawlessness, crime, repression, dishonesty, and graft, the work of the gospel is hindered. Because God wants all men to have the best opportunity to hear the truth, He favors good government, *"for this is good and acceptable in the sight of God our Savior."* So, what are we to do about it? We are to pray for it.

IF CHRISTIANS WOULD TAKE THE TIME THEY SPEND CRITICIZING THE GOVERNMENT TO PRAY FOR IT INSTEAD, THEY WOULD HAVE MUCH LESS TO CRITICIZE.

I have said many times that if Christians would take the time they spend criticizing the government to pray for it instead, they would have much less to criticize. Multitudes of citizens of most nations are not slow to criticize. In my opinion, sometimes the leaders of the government of a nation are more devoted to their task than most Christians of that nation are to doing their jobs as Christians. In those cases, we have little right to criticize the leaders, because we are failing in our responsibility to pray for them. And it is no small responsibility. It is a great responsibility.

When we pray for good government, what assurance does God give us? We find the answer in the first epistle of John:

> *Now this is the confidence that we have in Him, that if we ask anything according to His will, He hears us. And if we know that He hears us, whatever we ask, we know that we have the petitions that we have asked of Him.*
> (1 John 5:14–15)

The Greek term translated as *"confidence"* is a very strong word that actually means "complete confidence." This is not a questioning kind of faith but complete confidence in God. What is the nature of our confidence? Let me repeat: *"…that if we ask anything according to His will, He hears us. And if we know that He hears us, whatever we ask, we know that we have the petitions* [the requests] *that we have asked of Him."*

We know that good government is the will of God. So, if we pray for good government, we know that God hears us. And if we know that God hears us, we know we have the petition we asked for, which is good government. Here is the only possible conclusion: Either what the Bible says is unreliable, or we don't have good government because we don't pray for it. Which do you think is the right explanation?

My opinion is that Christians get bad government because they deserve it. By and large, I believe God's people get the kind of government they merit. I believe it is within the power of God's people to obtain good government for their nation. If they do not, what have they become? Salt that has lost its flavor. We are not doing the job we have been placed here to do.

ARE GOD'S PROMISES FOR TODAY?

We will shortly look at 2 Chronicles 7:14, which is a tremendous promise from the Word of God. However, some Christians think that the promises in the Old Testament do not apply today. So, before we delve into this verse, let's first remind ourselves of the following:

For all the promises of God in Him [Jesus Christ] are Yes, and in Him Amen, to the glory of God through us.   (2 Corinthians 1:20)

To whom does the phrase *"through us"* apply? That would be you and me. Without any question whatsoever, it refers to all Christians.

All the promises of God to all of us who have come to Him in Jesus Christ *"are"*—not *"were"* (past tense), not *"will be"* (future tense). They are right now *"Yes"* and *"Amen."*

According to this phrase, the promises of God have not come solely through the patriarchs, the apostles, or the early church. They have come *through us*—through you and me. We cannot get around that verse. It rules out all these fancy dispensational theories that apply all the "meat" to some previous or future age, leaving us nothing but the "bone" to gnaw upon in the present age. I do not believe that. It is *"through us."*

THE PROMISES
OF GOD HAVE NOT
COME SOLELY THROUGH
THE PATRIARCHS.
THEY HAVE COME
THROUGH US.

Some very close Christian friends of mine in Chicago who began as fundamentalists encountered a crisis. The wife became sick with an incurable condition of the kidney, and her specialist (who was an atheist) told her there was no hope for her kidney. So, she went to her fundamentalist bookstore to get a book on how to be healed. She admitted, "I came out with fourteen books on how to suffer, but not one on how to be healed."

Do you know what happened? These two dyed-in-the-wool fundamentalists, dotting every *i* and crossing every *t* of doctrine, went to a high Episcopal church in Wheaton, Illinois. The Episcopal rector anointed the wife with oil in the name of the Lord Jesus, and God instantly healed her. Why didn't the fundamentalists know about anointing with oil? Hadn't they read about it in the fifth chapter of the epistle of James, verses 14 and 15? Did that practice drop out of sight? No, they had "dispensationalized" it away.

So many times, we have cheated ourselves out of the best. We are living on skim milk when we are entitled to cream. As far as I am concerned, "All the promises of God in Christ are Yes, and in Him Amen, to the glory of God through me, Derek Prince." Let me put it this way: Every promise in the Bible that applies to my situation and meets my need is for me today. The same is true for you.

"IF MY PEOPLE"

With this truth about God's promises clearly in mind, let's examine 2 Chronicles 7:14. God said:

> *...if My people who are called by My name will humble themselves, and pray and seek My face, and turn from their wicked ways, then I will hear from heaven, and will forgive their sin and heal their land.*

He was saying, "If My people will do four things, I will do three things." Notice how His people are described: *"My people who are called by My name."* In the Hebrew, this phrase is literally "My people upon whom My name is called." If are you a Christian, the name of Christ is called upon you. This is the most exact description of Christians found anywhere in the Bible.

So, God says, "If My Christian people will do four things, I will do three." What are the four steps that God asks His people to take? (1) Humble themselves. (2) Pray. (3) Seek His face. (4) Turn from their wicked ways. If these four actions take place, then God promises He will hear from heaven, forgive their sins, and heal their land.

If the land of God's people does not get healed, has God failed to do what He has promised? Or have God's people failed to meet His conditions? Which do you believe is the correct explanation? Here is my assessment: There is nothing wrong with God. He always does what He has promised. If our land is not healed, it is because we have not met His four conditions.

Let's review these requirements. The first condition is to *humble ourselves.* Don't ask God to make you humble—you have to humble yourself. It is a decision you must make.

The second action is to *pray*, and we've been discussing how to go about this.

Third, we are to *seek God's face*. Don't just pray for ten minutes on Saturday evening. Pray until you get into the presence of almighty God. Believe me, you will know when you have touched God.

Fourth, *turn from our wicked ways*. The term *"wicked ways"* sometimes trips us up. You see, it is not the thief, the dropout, or the crack addict who holds back the hand of God. It is the wickedness found in the church. It is *our* wickedness. Most times, the problem is not so much what we do as what we do *not* do. We see this truth clearly in James 4:17:

> *Therefore, to him who knows to do good and does not do it, to him it is sin.*

In Matthew 25, we see another discussion about a failure to take the right action. This chapter talks about three types of people who will be banished forever from the presence of the Lord at His return: the foolish virgins, the unfaithful steward, and the goat nations. What did these people do that caused them to be banished forever from the presence of the Lord? I will answer that question in one word: *nothing*.

The foolish virgins did not take any oil; the unfaithful steward did nothing with his talent; and the goat nations ignored the hungry, thirsty, naked, and imprisoned. To them, Jesus said, *"Assuredly, I say to you, inasmuch as you did not do it to one of the least of these, you did not do it to Me"* (Matthew 25:45). The result? *"These will go away into everlasting punishment"* (verse 46). What a frightening thought! To be lost and damned forever for doing *nothing*!

In a similar vein, the prophet Samuel said to Saul and the children of Israel, *"Far be it from me that I should sin against the LORD in ceasing to pray for you"* (1 Samuel 12:23). He realized that ceasing to pray was a sin. It was "doing nothing."

PRAY AS GOD HAS COMMANDED

Here is our sobering conclusion: If our land is not healed, the fault lies with the church. We have not met God's conditions. It is not God who has changed or failed to keep His promise. We are the culprits. If we do not repent and meet God's conditions so that He, in turn, can heal our land, then our designation is salt that has lost its flavor. We are then good for nothing but to be thrown out and trampled underfoot by men. What a terrible shame if that should happen!

However, I do not believe it needs to happen. The alternative is that we, the church, will repent. The alternative is for us to pray as God has commanded.

In chapter 10, we established that prayer is the great powerhouse of the world. So, in the next chapter, I am going to give you some personal examples of prayer that changed the course of history—prayers offered by myself and others. I will give you exact and detailed accounts, which I believe will greatly encourage you.

However, to properly respond to the truths we have examined in this chapter, let's close with a prayer of repentance.

Father, we come to You now in the name of the Lord Jesus Christ. First of all, like Daniel, we confess our sins and the sins of our people. We confess that we have failed You, Lord, and that we have failed our people. We are sorry, and we ask You to forgive us. We pray that You will help us to repent and so to change our ways, in order that the nation in which we live may be transformed. O Lord, please heal our land. In Jesus' name we pray. Amen.

CHAPTER 13

BECAUSE WE PRAYED

Let us once again read Matthew 5:13. By now, you should know how we will read this verse. Without changing the meaning, we make it personal:

> We are the salt of the earth; but if the salt loses its flavor, how shall it be seasoned? We are then good for nothing but to be thrown out and trampled underfoot by men.

CONDITIONS FOR ANSWERED PRAYER

Before I share with you some of my own personal testimonies of prayer that has impacted history, I think it would be helpful to recap what we have learned so far in this book.

I have pointed out to you the main reason why the church is the decisive factor in world affairs. What is that reason? The church can participate in a spiritual conflict with the spiritual forces that influence the destiny of men and nations. There is *no other agency on earth* that can participate in this spiritual conflict. Again, Paul spoke of this warfare in Ephesians 6:12:

> *For we do not wrestle against flesh and blood, but against principalities, against powers, against the rulers of the darkness of this age, against spiritual hosts of wickedness in the heavenly places.*

We have seen that God has provided us with the means of victory in the spiritual realm. The basis of all victory is found in Colossians 2:15:

> *Having disarmed principalities and powers, He [Christ Jesus] made a public spectacle of them, triumphing over them in it [the cross].*

At the cross, Jesus Christ already accomplished the total defeat of all these spiritual enemies. Now, what you and I are asked to do as His representatives in His name is to apply His victory and make it effective. The working out of the victory that Christ has won is left to you and me as His church—the members of His body, His personal representatives.

We also have understood that because we are called to spiritual warfare, God has provided us with an arsenal of spiritual weapons, vividly described by Paul in 2 Corinthians:

> *For the weapons of our warfare are not carnal but mighty in God for pulling down strongholds, casting down arguments and every high thing that exalts itself against the knowledge of God, bringing every thought into captivity to the obedience of Christ.* (2 Corinthians 10:4–5)

We explored what I consider to be some of our major spiritual weapons. I will mention them here again briefly: prayer, fasting, praise, testimony, preaching, and the supernatural gifts of the Spirit (which, as we noted previously, are also important weapons, though we will not discuss them further for the purposes of this study).

We then examined in more depth "the great powerhouse of the world," which is our first spiritual weapon—prayer. We began with the words of Jesus contained in three verses in Matthew 18:

> *Assuredly, I say to you, whatever you bind on earth will be bound in heaven, and whatever you loose on earth will be loosed in heaven. Again I say to you that if two of you agree on earth concerning anything that they ask, it will be done for them by My Father in heaven. For where two or three are gathered together in My name, I am there in the midst of them.* (Matthew 18:18–20)

This passage describes what I call "the secret place of all power." Nothing is omitted; no need is left out. In that place, you can accomplish anything you need to achieve in prayer. God's omnipotence is made available to you. We know that Jesus said, *"With God all things are possible"* (Mark 10:27). But He also said, *"All things are possible to him who believes"* (Mark 9:23).

In other words, through your faith, God's omnipotence is made available to you. But I also pointed out to you that this secret place of all power is protected and fenced in. That fence is in the form of right relationships. You will not have access to this power unless you have carefully cultivated and maintained right relationships with every other person, as far as it lies within your power. If you have a poor relationship with other people—for instance, an attitude of resentment or bitterness or unforgiveness—you do not qualify for the administration of this power.

PATTERNS, PROGRAMS, PROCESSES

We then saw that we are given a specific pattern and program of prayer in 1 Timothy. Let's examine that passage again.

> *Therefore I exhort first of all that supplications, prayers, intercessions, and giving of thanks be made for all men, for kings and all who are in authority, that we may lead a quiet and peaceable life in all godliness and reverence. For this is good and acceptable in the sight of God our Savior, who desires all men to be saved and to come to the knowledge of the truth.* (1 Timothy 2:1–4)

The first activity in the corporate life of the church is prayer. And what is the first item on the prayer list? Verse 2 indicates the answer: *"kings and all who are in authority."*

In two words, what are we to pray for? Good government. And the reason? *"That we may lead a quiet and peaceable life in all godliness and reverence"* (1 Timothy 2:2).

Is this the will of God? Scripture makes it clear that it is: *"For this is good and acceptable in the sight of God our Savior"* (1 Timothy 2:3).

Why does God approve good government? Because the environment it provides is most conducive to His goal: "[He] *desires all men to be saved and to come to the knowledge of the truth*" (1 Timothy 2:4).

Clearly, God wants a favorable state of affairs in which there is maximum freedom to bring the truth of the gospel to all people. Without a doubt, good government actually facilitates the work of preaching the gospel.

What is the end result of these prayers? Scripture tells us that if we pray for anything we know to be in the will of God, we have the assurance of receiving what we have prayed for:

> *Now this is the confidence that we have in Him* [remember, the word "confidence" is a very strong word meaning "complete confidence"], *that if we ask anything according to His will, He hears us. And if we know that He hears us, whatever we ask, we know that we have the petitions that we have asked of Him.*   (1 John 5:14–15)

GOOD GOVERNMENT
IS THE WILL OF
GOD; THEREFORE,
IF WE PRAY FOR
GOOD GOVERNMENT,
WE KNOW
GOD HEARS US.

When we pray according to the will of God, we know God hears us. Further, if we know God hears us, we know we have the petitions we have asked of Him.

The logic of this entire process is so clear and encouraging. Good government is explicitly stated to be the will of God; therefore, if we pray for good government, we know God hears us. And if we know God hears us, we know our petition for good government has been granted. So, if we do not have good government, what is the reason? We have not prayed. Further, if we fail to pray, we have become salt that has lost its flavor. We are no longer doing our job in the earth.

This process is clarified in 2 Chronicles, where God gives this specific promise to the people on whom His name is called:

...if My people who are called by My name will humble themselves, and pray and seek My face, and turn from their wicked ways, then I will hear from heaven, and will forgive their sin and heal their land.

(2 Chronicles 7:14)

The last phrase is crucial: God has promised He will heal our land. If our land is not healed, the reason is that we have not met the four conditions God has outlined, which are to humble ourselves, pray, seek God's face, and turn from our wicked ways. It is not the sin of the unconverted or the unchurched that is the problem. It is the sin of God's people that is holding back revival and cleansing for a nation.

A few final conclusions. Scripture says, *"For the time has come for judgment to begin at the house of God"* (1 Peter 4:17). That is where God's judgment always begins. If God's people will submit to judgment, then the way is open for God's blessing to flow out to the world. Here is a wonderful statement made by Evan Roberts, a key figure in the Welsh Revival of 1904: "Bend the church and bow the world." This saying is still true today. Wherever God can bend His church, He has no problem in bowing the world. The problem is the church. It always has been.

PERSONAL EXAMPLES OF ANSWERED PRAYER

Now I would like to share with you some personal examples of answered prayer in matters of international affairs. These are prayers I have seen specifically answered. Some may think I am boasting by recounting these experiences. I assure you that I am not. When we come to the question of prayer, we are left with two possibilities—and only two. Either God *does* answer prayer or He *does not*. If God does answer prayer, you are silly *not* to pray. But if God does not answer prayer, you are silly *to* pray. It is up to you to decide which you believe. As for me and my house, we believe God answers prayer. (See Joshua 24:15.) When we have prayed for a matter specifically in the name of Jesus, and it has happened, we have accepted that happening with thankfulness as the answer to our prayers.

VICTORY IN THE BATTLE OF EL ALAMEIN

The first example I am going to provide happened during the Second World War. It was when I was a British soldier in the North African desert, newly saved and baptized in the Holy Spirit. My unit was part of what was called the Western Desert Force of the British Army, which later became the well-known Eighth Army.

"LORD, GIVE US LEADERS SUCH THAT IT WILL BE FOR YOUR GLORY TO GIVE US VICTORY THROUGH THEM."

At that time, I was absolutely appalled by the behavior and standards of the British officers. They were selfish, undisciplined, and irresponsible, so the men had no confidence in them and would not willingly work with them. The result of such behavior was an army that was divided against itself—which, as the Scriptures clearly say, cannot stand. (See, for example, Matthew 12:25.) Consequently, we had the dubious privilege of taking part in the longest continuous retreat ever recorded in the history of the British Army, from a place called El Agheila in Libya (or Tripoli) to El Alamein in Egypt—a distance of approximately fifteen hundred miles.

I saw the gravity of the situation, and I longed to pray. I also longed for a British victory. Yet I thought to myself, *How can I expect God to give victory with leadership like this?* However, a specific prayer came into my mind, and I want you to take careful note of what I prayed, because it is just as applicable today. Here was my prayer at that time: "Lord, give us leaders such that it will be for Your glory to give us victory through them." I want to repeat this prayer, because its wording is very significant: "Lord, give us leaders such that it will be for Your glory to give us victory through them."

Now I will tell you how God answered my prayer. First, the British government decided to change the command of the Eighth Army. They relieved the commander and chose another man, whose name was Gott. He was an officer up at the front line, and he was flown back to the base at Cairo to take command. As his plane landed, however, it overturned. Gott was thrown out of the plane and broke his neck. Suddenly, the British government had to find a commander for this critical situation and this pivotal theater of the conflict.

In response, Winston Churchill, more or less on his own initiative, looked around and picked a comparatively unknown young officer named Montgomery. Without anyone planning it, and contrary to everyone's expectation, Montgomery was suddenly promoted to command the Eighth Army.

I want to tell you a significant fact about Montgomery. He was a born-again Christian. His father was a bishop of the Church of England and Secretary of the Society for Propagating the Gospel. No one knew much about Montgomery, but his first official act was to tighten up the discipline in the British Army. He brought the officers into line, changing the morale and the *esprit de corps* of the entire force. It was just after this that the decisive battle of El Alamein was fought. El Alamein was the first real major victory for the Allies in the entire course of the war. Winston Churchill called it "the end of the beginning." Certainly, it was a major turning point.

The day after the Battle of El Alamein was fought, I was in the western desert with a group of soldiers, standing around a truck. On the tailboard of the truck was a little radio. Out of this radio came the voice of a news commentator describing the preparations that had gone on before the actual fighting of the Battle of El Alamein. In his report, this news commentator described how General Montgomery, the commander of the Allied forces, publicly said before his men and his officers, "Let us ask the Lord, mighty in battle, to give us the victory."

When I heard those words coming out of that radio, it was as if heaven's electricity went through my body from the crown of my head to the soles of my feet. It was as if God said, *That is the answer to your prayer.* This is one example of a prayer that had significant, widespread impact.

THE DEFENSE OF JERUSALEM

A few years later, my wife Lydia and I were in Jewish Jerusalem when the State of Israel came into being on May 15, 1948. When statehood was announced, Jewish Jerusalem was besieged by five Arab armies. The entire little State of Israel, on the day that it became a nation, had war declared on it by the five surrounding Arab nations. Two million Jews were facing about forty million well-armed Arabs who were intent on pushing the Jews into the sea and annihilating them.

Prior to that event, my wife had spent almost twenty years in Jerusalem. She had been through many of the previous riots, commotions, and conflicts, and she had seen that the Jews had been totally unprepared to defend themselves. She had seen them tie bread knives onto the staves of brooms as rudimentary weapons. She had witnessed little Jewish babies having their arms torn off and being thrown down from the roofs of buildings.

As a matter of fact, shortly before the State of Israel came into being, we were living in a particular building in the center of Jerusalem. Our daughter Elizabeth, who was only four and who was our youngest girl at the time, came to me one day and said, "Daddy, Daddy. There are a lot of dead men in the street." I went to the window, and this is what I saw: a patrol of young Jewish volunteers (they were not really men and women but mere boys and girls) who had been ambushed outside of Jerusalem by a group of Arabs. The Arabs had killed them and then cut them up into small pieces—and when I say small pieces, I mean smaller than your hand. A British truck had been sent out to gather up these bodies, and it had brought them into the center of Jerusalem just outside our house. The truck was delivering them for transfer to a Jewish ambulance to take them away for burial. To add to the horrific sight, I saw a person using a piece of a gasoline can to scrape a little bit of human remains off the pavement and dump it into the back of an ambulance.

That awful incident gave me firsthand evidence of what to expect if the Arabs should prevail at that time in their attempt to capture Jerusalem. Without being melodramatic, I can state as an actual fact that every Jewish mother was advised to keep a loaded revolver with one bullet for each of her daughters and one more for herself. The directive was to use it if the city was taken by the Arabs.

In the midst of this grave situation, my wife and I turned to God in prayer. We were praying together against the background of what I have told you. Not wanting to sound nationalistic or prejudiced, I will report what my wife prayed. I heard her say this: "Lord, paralyze the Arabs." Soon after the announcement of statehood, the fighting developed into open war in Jerusalem. The Haganah, the Jewish volunteer army, asked our permission to set up an outpost in our backyard. I knew they would set it up whether we said yes or no, so I politely said yes. There they were, settled into our backyard, so we gradually got acquainted with these young Jewish men. When the first ceasefire was imposed by the United Nations after almost two months of fighting, these young men would come into our living room and talk with us. They had been right in the center of much of the fighting that had taken place.

One day, they were talking to us in our living room, and they said, "You know, it is most remarkable. We go into a building or some other place of confrontation, and the Arabs far outnumber us. They are far better armed, and yet they seem unable to do anything. It is just as if they were paralyzed."

In our very own home, that young man used the specific word that Lydia had prayed. Do you see how good God is? Not only does He answer our prayer, but He can also let us know that He has answered our prayer in the most specific, authentic, up-to-date way.

THE DEATH OF STALIN

I am going to move on a few years to the 1950s, when Lydia and I were the directors of a Christian mission in London, England. We were still very interested in and concerned for the Jewish people. At a certain point, we received reliable news from Russia that Stalin was planning a fresh persecution of the Jews there. We were not directly involved with ministry to Russia at that time. However, as I said, we were concerned for God's people Israel. There was a little group that used to meet in our mission for prayer, and we knew some other groups up and down the country—groups of Spirit-filled people who were burdened for Israel. So, we agreed among ourselves that we would set aside a certain day for prayer and fasting on behalf of the Jewish people in Russia.

We did just that—and what was the outcome? Less than two weeks from the day when we prayed and fasted, Stalin was dead. We did not ask God to kill Stalin. (You don't have to tell God what to do. He knows.) But I am sure you will agree with me that Stalin's death marked a total change in Russian policy. We now speak about the era of "de-Stalinization," which started with the death of Stalin. Why did it start then? I believe it was because we prayed.

A STABLE AND PROSPEROUS KENYA

Lydia and I were in East Africa—in Kenya—for five years, from 1957 through 1961. When we went out to that country to direct a mission there, it was British East Africa. When we left, it was separating into three nations and moving toward independence from Britain.

As one of those three nations, Kenya was due to receive independence in the next year or two. It had been torn asunder by the Mau Mau revolt, which I won't attempt to describe in detail except to say that it was one of the most fearful and bestial outbreaks you could ever imagine. The Congo (to the west of Kenya) had received independence just prior to that time, and it had immediately been plunged into destructive civil war. Many of the full gospel missionaries who had escaped from the Congo came and took refuge in our mission station for quite a while.

At that time, all the political and social experts were of the opinion that Kenya was going to go the way of the Congo—but in a far worse way. Every influence contributing to civil strife and destruction in the Congo was present in Kenya, except to a more intensified degree.

In 1960, right in the midst of this unsettled situation, Lydia and I took part in a conference of two hundred young African students and teachers, along with a team of missionaries. We were gathered for about a week, and on Sunday evening, the last service of the conference was held. The meeting lasted for four hours. After one of the other missionaries preached, the Spirit of the Lord moved mightily. The last two hours of that service were not under the control of any human being. They were under the control of the Holy Spirit.

During that latter period, I had the impression we had touched God and that His power was now available to us. As I relate the thought that came to me, I want to preface it by saying that I am not being critical of the Pentecostal movement. (At that time, I had been a Pentecostal for at least twelve years.) But this thought came to me: *Now, let's not do as Pentecostal people sometimes do and just squander this power in selfish spiritual self-enjoyment. Let's use it for the purpose for which God made it available.* Another thought came to me out of the Scriptures, just as I have presented it to you in this book—that the Christians in a land are responsible for the destiny of their own country. There in that meeting were the pick of the crop of some young, Christian future leaders of Kenya, and it was their responsibility to pray for the future of their land.

I made my way to the platform with the intention of challenging those young people to pray for the future of Kenya. As I did, I walked past Lydia, who was sitting in another section. She put out her hand and stopped me. I said, "What is it?" and she said, "Tell them to pray for Kenya." I answered, "That is just what I am going to the platform to do." Because of what Lydia had said, I knew I had the mind of the Lord.

As I came to the podium, I silenced those two hundred young people and told them, in essence, about the responsibility of Christians to pray for the government of their land. I said, "We are in contact with heaven. Now is the time for you Africans to pray for the future of your country."

Then I led them in a prayer—and, believe me, they prayed! Something happened. I knew it immediately. The spiritual atmosphere of Kenya was changed, and it would never be altogether the same from that hour of prayer.

Beside me on the platform was a young man who was an interpreter for the missionary who had been the first speaker in the meeting. This young interpreter had graduated from our college and had already taken a teaching position. He was kneeling beside me as we prayed. When we finished, he stood up and said, "I would like to tell you what God showed me while we were praying." (For years, I kept a document of what he said—written out, dated, and signed by that young man.) Here is what the young man told me: "While we were praying, I saw a red horse. It was very fierce, and it was coming toward Kenya from the east. There was a very black man sitting on it, and behind it were other horses—also red, and also fierce—coming toward Kenya." (I doubt that this young man had ever read the prophet Zechariah, but the picture that the Holy Spirit gave him was absolutely parallel to the scriptural description in Zechariah 1:7–8.)

Next, he said, "While we were praying, I saw these horses turn around and move away from Kenya, heading instead up toward the north. And while I was wondering what this meant, God spoke to me. This is what God said: *Only the supernatural power of the prayer of My people can turn away the troubles that are coming upon Kenya.*"

There is a reason I am quoting word for word what that young man said: if you change *Kenya* to the name of your own country, you need not change one other word. *Only the supernatural power of the prayer of My people can turn away the troubles that are coming upon* [substitute the name of your nation].

How did events turn out in Kenya? I will just say that in the years that have elapsed since that prophetic word, everything has happened exactly as God showed that young man it would. Shortly after Kenya gained independence, the communists made a determined, planned attempt to take over the country. They came in from the east, from the island of Madagascar. The agents they used had been trained in Cuba, and some of them spoke Spanish. They succeeded in getting into Tanzania, the country south of Kenya. But in a most unexpected way, Jomo Kenyatta, the president of Kenya, stopped them short, turned them out, and refused to allow the country to fall under their control. In fact, he took a very strong stand against communism, as well as against Russian and Chinese infiltration, and he dismissed one of his right-hand leaders publicly with ignominy because he had been involved in receiving financial assistance from Red China. Today, most commentators would agree that contrary to all expectations, Kenya is probably the most stable and prosperous of all the nearly fifty new nations that have been formed in Africa since World War II.

Some years ago, I picked up a sixteen-page supplement to the *London Times* that was devoted entirely to a summary of Kenya since independence. The conclusion of the article was that Kenya was the most orderly, the most successful, and the most hopeful of all the newly emerging African nations. Years later, I received a letter from missionary friends in various countries of East Africa. They said: "The brightest spot is Kenya. It is a center for missionary expansion from outside. The government of Kenya is far more favorable to Christian missionary activity than any of the other governments in the whole of that area."

Why did that happen? I believe it took place because we prayed. Facing those dire circumstances, we would have been very silly *not* to pray, wouldn't we? May I say that the same is true for you? In the circumstances you presently face, if you do not pray, you will be very silly as well, won't you?

THE VITAL ROLE OF THE SPIRIT

As sinners, we have nothing good to give God except what He has first given us. We have nothing of ourselves that is worth giving to God. This is equally true in prayer, but most people fail to realize it. You have nothing to pray to God about that is worth praying until God first gives it to you by the Holy Spirit. Only then is it good to pray.

> *Likewise the Spirit also helps in our weaknesses. For we do not know what we should pray for as we ought, but the Spirit Himself makes intercession for us with groanings which cannot be uttered. Now He who searches the hearts knows what the mind of the Spirit is, because He makes intercession for the saints according to the will of God.*
> (Romans 8:26–27)

This passage reminds us that, in ourselves, we really do not know how to pray. "*We do not know what we should pray for as we ought*" (Romans 8:26). Left to ourselves, without the Holy Spirit, we are incapable of praying aright. This is an infirmity shared by the entire human race. The only time we can pray effectively is when the Holy Spirit comes to our help and gives us a prayer.

Let me explain one other aspect of the Spirit's work: revelation. Are you aware that you can look at situations and not see them until the Holy Spirit shows them to you? You can look right at something that should be obvious and not see it until the Holy Spirit illuminates it. Many years ago, a remarkable thought came to me. I was thinking of the world situation, and it occurred to me that a vast block of hundreds of millions of people united under atheistic communism simply could not help being a hindrance to the purposes of God in the world. You may have some fanciful way of explaining that away, but I do not. To me, it was a hindrance—a block. That situation was not inspired by God but by the devil. Please understand that I am not speaking with bias or in a prejudicial way against any specific nation.

When this realization came, I thought to myself, *Well, how do we pray against that hindrance?* Immediately, there came to me a prayer that David had prayed when he was faced with political opposition and persecution. You will find his prayer in Psalm 55:9: *"Destroy, O Lord, and divide their tongues."* Off and on, as I felt prompted by the Holy Spirit concerning the entire Communist Bloc, I would pray this prayer. In fact, I did so for quite a number of years. My prayer would be something like this: "Lord, with regard to those who deliberately and knowingly oppose You, Your Christ, Your Spirit, Your Word, Your people, and Your purposes in the earth [by that time, I had them pretty well identified], I am praying as Your servant David prayed: *'Destroy, O Lord, and divide their tongues.'"*

I viewed that as an inspired prayer because it went to the very core of the whole situation. If their tongues were divided—turned against one another—they could not take care of themselves.

As I consistently prayed that prayer, these were some of the results I saw. First of all, Russia and China split from one another. They spent much more of their time abusing and vilifying one another than they did any of the rest of the world.

Then I saw an extended period with evidence of very strong internal strife inside Red China. I also saw clear activity in which the satellite nations of Eastern Europe did their best to break away from Soviet Russia (culminating in the actual disintegration of the Soviet Union itself). I just kept on praying, "Lord, thank You for what You have done. Destroy and divide their tongues." My belief is that the enemies of God were fighting among themselves because we had prayed Psalm 55:9: *"Destroy, O Lord, and divide their tongues."*

RESISTING IN PRAYER

Many years ago, even before the Vietnam conflict developed fully, it came to my mind that the situation there could not be the will of God. Furthermore, I felt that it could not be the will of God that the whole of Southeast Asia should be submerged under bloodshed and strife and atheistic communism. So I said to myself, *If that situation in Vietnam is not the will of God, why don't you pray about it?* As a result, I took on the responsibility to pray about Vietnam, even though, at the time, I was not an American citizen. In the following paragraph, I will spell out how I felt directed to pray.

Let me first remind you again of what we have discussed in previous chapters. We concluded that every one of the spiritual weapons we use is effective only insofar as we recognize that we are using it to administer the victory Christ has already won over the principalities and powers. I did not necessarily have a set pattern of prayer to administer the victory Jesus had won. However, I will use the case of Vietnam as an example of how I would pray.

WE HAVE AN OBLIGATION TO CONTINUALLY RESIST THE ENCROACHMENTS OF SATAN IN ANY PART OF THE WORLD TO WHICH THE HOLY SPIRIT DIRECTS OUR ATTENTION.

I would say: "Lord, You know about Southeast Asia. You know the principalities and powers in the unseen realm that are ruling and dominating, seeking to destroy, to plunge that nation into bloodshed, and to bring down a veil of spiritual darkness over the area. God, I do not believe this is Your will. In the name of Jesus, on the basis of the finished work of Calvary, because Christ has already defeated these principalities and powers, I stand against them and I demand that they withdraw. I resist you, Satan, in the name of Jesus. I further declare that the Bible, which is the Word of God, says that if I resist you, Satan, you will have to flee from me." I believe that the Lord's direction for me to pray in that way is a good pattern that can be used in praying for your own nation or any other nation.

Please be assured that I do not flatter myself into thinking that if I pray that prayer once, it is going to change the whole situation. The command in the Bible is in the continuous present tense: *"Resist the devil* [continually] *and he will flee from you"* (James 4:7). I believe that you and I have an obligation to continually resist the encroachments of Satan in any part of the world to which the Holy Spirit directs our attention. Whenever the Holy Spirit shows us that what is taking place is not the will of God, we have the authority to administer Christ's victory and call for it to stop. Not just a single prayer, but continual prayer with determination and perseverance.

An additional point is not to simply pray alone but to call for some reinforcements. We need to recognize that we will not get the job done by ourselves. That is what I believe. Also, we cannot afford to accept defeat, because the next battle we fight may be waged much closer to home—both in the material realm and in the spiritual realm.

THE NATIONS: OUR INHERITANCE

To broaden our perspective on this theme, let me point out three verses from Psalm 2. I referred to these verses earlier when I spoke about Jesus, our Representative, meeting Satan on the cross, defeating him, and rising again. We noted that Jesus is our risen Head who has become the First Begotten from the dead and the Prince, or Ruler, of the kings of the earth. Scripture speaks of this prophetically in the passage below. While men were rejecting Jesus Christ, crying "Crucify Him," condemning Him, sending Him to the cross, and sealing Him away in the tomb, this is what God was saying:

"Yet I have set My King on My holy hill of Zion." [The Son then responds and says:] *"I will declare the decree: the LORD has said to Me, 'You are My Son, today I have begotten You* [from the dead]. [The Father

continues:] *Ask of Me, and I will give You the nations* [the Gentiles] *for Your inheritance, and the ends of the earth for Your possession.'"*

(Psalm 2:6–8)

On the basis of what Christ did through His death and resurrection, the nations, or Gentiles, and the uttermost parts of the earth have become His legally entitled inheritance. However, it is my belief that Scripture does not leave it only to Jesus to do all the asking. As the body of Christ—the church—we are placed under an obligation to ask the Father to give Christ His rightful inheritance in the nations. We are to apply the victory of Calvary in prayer in such a way that the doors are open for the whole Gentile world—the whole un-evangelized world—to hear about Jesus Christ and to have the opportunity to accept Him as Savior and to crown Him as Lord.

THE HIGH PRAISES

In Psalm 149, we find yet another revelation of the power and the responsibility of God's people in relation to this spiritual conflict we are discussing:

> *Let the saints be joyful in glory; let them sing aloud on their beds. Let the high praises of God be in their mouth, and a two-edged sword in their hand.* (Psalm 149:5–6)

The saints are always *"joyful in glory."* When the glory comes down, people get joyful.

Please notice the two spiritual weapons mentioned here: praise and the two-edged sword of the Word of God. How are we to use them?

> *To execute vengeance on the nations, and punishments on the peoples; to bind their kings with chains, and their nobles with fetters of iron; to execute on them the written judgment; this honor have all His saints. Praise the LORD!* (Psalm 149:7–9)

Do you see clearly that this is the honor, or privilege, that has been accorded to all the saints of God through Jesus Christ? By high praises, by prayer, by the sharp, two-edged sword of the Word, we are to execute God's judgment on the rulers of the darkness of this world—to bind them with chains and with fetters of iron by prayer in such a way that their kingdoms can be spoiled and their captives liberated and taken from them. *"This honor have all His saints."* You are one of those saints. You are entitled to join in this activity: *"To execute on them the written judgment."*

BY HIGH PRAISES, BY PRAYER, BY THE WORD, WE ARE TO EXECUTE GOD'S JUDGMENT ON THE RULERS OF THE DARKNESS OF THIS WORLD.

We see a confirmation of this truth in the twelfth chapter of John, in which Jesus spoke of His coming death on the cross. In verse 31, He expressed one of the victories He was about to accomplish by His crucifixion: *"Now is the judgment of this world; now the ruler of this world will be cast out."* How was the ruler of this world to be cast out? We see the answer in John 12:32: *"And I, if I am lifted up from the earth...."* How would the ruler of this world be cast out? Through the cross.

Please understand that through the cross, this world has been brought to judgment in the sight of God. The prince of this world has been cast out and rendered powerless on the basis of what Christ did on our behalf through His shed blood, His atoning death, and His triumphant resurrection. Because Jesus has ascended into heaven, He has left it to you and me to obtain the inheritance for Him, to apply the victory, and to drive our spiritual enemies out of their positions.

MAKE SATAN NERVOUS

Concerning the power that God's people are to have against the enemy, Jesus made this statement:

> *And I also say to you that you are Peter, and on this rock I will build My church, and the gates of Hades ["hell" KJV] shall not prevail against it.*
>
> (Matthew 16:18)

Most Christians interpret this verse as follows: "Well, here we are, beleaguered and besieged inside the city. Maybe, if God is really good to us, the gates will hold out and Satan won't be able to get in." If that is how you understand this verse, you couldn't be further from the truth. The real picture is totally opposite of this typical view. When the church is built upon the Rock, Christ Jesus, then it can go out and storm the gates of hell. And the gates of hell cannot keep the church out.

We find one of the great messianic promises to Abraham and to his seed in Genesis 22:17: "*And your descendants shall possess the gate of their enemies.*" We are the descendants, the "*seed of Abraham*" (Hebrews 2:16), through faith in Jesus Christ. We have a legal, scriptural right to storm the gates of hell, to take them and possess them in the name of Jesus.

There is nothing that makes the devil more afraid than the prospect of the saints of God discovering this fact and starting to do it. As we discussed in an earlier chapter, this is Satan's most guarded secret. There is nothing that he wants to keep from you and me more than this truth: It is up to us, and it is in our power, to administer the defeat Christ has already inflicted. I believe both heaven and hell are waiting for us to do it.

What about you? Do you intend to do something about it? If your answer to this question is yes—if you want to put this truth into action—please declare these words out loud:

> Lord, I believe that through the death of Jesus on the cross, the victory over our enemy has already been won. I declare that it is now up to me and all Your saints to administer this defeat of principalities and powers, which Jesus has secured through His triumph.
>
> In Your strength, and by Your Spirit, I will walk in that triumph, obtaining the inheritance of the nations of the world and applying the power of the blood of Jesus to drive out our enemies before us. Amen!

CHAPTER 14

GOING THE DISTANCE

In this chapter, I want to bring together two major themes. The first topic, which we have already covered, designates Jesus Christ as *"the last Adam"* (1 Corinthians 15:45) and *"the second Man"* (verse 47). I pointed out that in the divine plan, Jesus was the end of one race and the beginning of another. As the last Adam, He took upon Himself the sin, the transgression, the condemnation, and the total failure of the Adamic race. By His atoning death, He expiated the guilt of Adam's race. And by His resurrection into newness of life, He opened the way for the initiation of a new race, of which He is the Head.

The apostle Peter wrote, *"Blessed be the God and Father of our Lord Jesus Christ, who according to His abundant mercy has begotten us again to a living hope through the resurrection of Jesus Christ from the dead"* (1 Peter 1:3). As we follow Him through His death and into His resurrection by faith and identification with Him, we become members of this new race.

The new race is called *"one new man"* (Ephesians 2:15). This *"new man"* is destined by God to fulfill the purpose that Adam failed to fulfill. Adam was created in the likeness and image of God to show forth God's likeness to creation and to exercise God's authority on His behalf. Adam was created to exercise dominion. Yet he lost his dominion and became a slave to Satan and sin when he obeyed the devil rather than God.

BRINGING THE TWO THEMES TOGETHER

THEME 1: REGAINING WHAT WAS LOST

It is important for us to recognize that Jesus has fully dealt with the legal issue of Adam's failure. When Jesus appeared after the resurrection and revealed Himself to His disciples, He said, *"All authority has been given to Me"* (Matthew 28:18). Essentially, He was saying, "What you lost, I have regained."

On that basis, He further said, *"Go therefore and make disciples of all the nations"* (Matthew 28:19). In other words, "Be the administrators of My authority. Demonstrate My power. Fulfill My purposes. I'm going back to heaven. In My place, I will send you another Comforter, the Holy Spirit. And when you receive Him in His might, you will go forth under His direction and leadership to accomplish what the first Adam failed to do. You will be My visible representatives. You will be able to say, as I said, *'He who has seen Me has seen the Father.'* As I came to do My Father's will, you will go to do My will. As I testified of the Father that it was He dwelling in Me who did the works, you will testify of Me that it is Christ dwelling in you doing the works. As I testified of the Father that I spoke not My own words but the words that the Father gave Me, you will testify, 'We do not speak our own words but the words that Christ gave us.' This is My plan. As My Father sent Me, I also send you." (See John 5:30; 12:49; 14:9–10, 12, 16–17; 20:21.)

WE ARE REPRESENTATIVES OF JESUS CHRIST, WITH SPECIAL AUTHORITY, SENT FORTH FROM HEAVEN'S GOVERNMENT TO ACCOMPLISH HEAVEN'S WILL.

As the disciples of Jesus, we are ambassadors for Christ. Second Corinthians 5:19 declares this truth: *"God was in Christ reconciling the world to Himself, not imputing their trespasses to them, and has committed to us the word of reconciliation."* Verse 20 begins, *"Now then, we are ambassadors for Christ…."* We are representatives of Jesus Christ, with special authority, sent forth from heaven's government to accomplish heaven's will.

This is one aspect of the first of the two themes that I want to bring together in this chapter. I am going to try to make this teaching as practical as I can. Through the years, I have come to the conclusion that if a truth is not practical, it is not spiritual. God does not promote something that will not work. Conversely, anything that God does promote will work. God is the most practical Person in the entire universe. What He promises and promotes will work.

THEME 2: BRINGING PEOPLE FROM DESOLATION TO RESTORATION

Second, I want to focus on a topic that is the main theme of the prophet Joel: restoration in place of desolation. As I understand it, Joel is the prophet of this great last-day outpouring of the Holy Spirit upon all flesh. It was the book of Joel from which Peter quoted on the day of Pentecost: *"But this is what was spoken by the prophet Joel: 'And it shall come to pass in the last days…'"* (Acts 2:16–17). From those initial words, he took Joel's prophecy right down to the end of time. Continuing in verse 20, Peter talked about what would happen before the *"great and awesome day of the LORD"* comes: *"'The sun shall be turned into darkness, and the moon into blood.'"* In Peter's words, we find Joel's prophecy as it refers to the close of this age.

What descended on the early church was the first rain. What is falling today is the latter rain, immediately prior to the harvest. This is very clear. Dispensationally, I believe there is no problem with this crystal clear outline, in miniature, of church history. Looking back over twenty centuries, we can see that it has been exactly as the prophet Joel said it would be. I am absolutely convinced that we are in the days of the latter rain, the days of the great outpouring spoken of by Joel.

If I were to sum up the theme of Joel in my own words, I would say it is desolation followed by restoration followed by judgment. The scene opens with total desolation, the most total picture of utter desolation you can conceive. As you read chapter one of Joel for yourself, you will see that there is nothing that has not been desolated.

Then, in the second chapter comes the promise: *"I will restore to you..."* (Joel 2:25). And the restoration is effected by the outpouring of the Holy Spirit.

In the third chapter, we find these words:

Multitudes, multitudes in the valley of decision! For the day of the L*ORD* *is near in the valley of decision.* (Joel 3:14)

The outpouring of the Spirit brings man face-to-face with God's judgment. There is no room left for neutrality when the Spirit has been poured out. This is why so many people shun and run away from the moving of the Spirit. He rules out neutrality.

When the Spirit of God really comes to work, you must make a decision. That is what is going to happen before this age closes. Multitudes from all nations will be brought down into the valley of decision, and they will not leave that valley until they have made a decision.

The decision is simple: it is for or against Jesus Christ—that is all. Jesus said, *"He who is not with Me is against Me"* (Matthew 12:30).

A RESTORATION PARALLEL

In the forefront of Joel's prophecy, you will notice two "trees": the vine and the fig tree. I have always understood these two trees to be the two types of God's people in the earth: the vine, typifying the church; and the fig tree, typifying Israel. I believe this perspective links up very clearly with the words of Jesus:

Then He spoke to them a parable: "Look at the fig tree, and all the trees. [Jesus was referring to the first chapter of Joel, verses 12 and 19, which talk about *"all the trees of the field."*] *When they are already budding, you see and know for yourselves that summer is now near."* (Luke 21:29–30)

The desolation is ending; the harvest is coming. Some years ago, God showed me that the restoration of the two trees had begun and was proceeding exactly parallel in time. Just about the time that we began to hear about the outpouring of the Holy Spirit upon the church in this last measure, we heard of the political restoration of Israel, which is a fantastically interesting subject. In 1897, the first Zionist World Conference was held in Basel, Switzerland. In 1904, the founder of Zionism, Theodore Hertzel, died. He was called a visionary and a dreamer, but he said, "Within fifty years what you call a dream will be a fulfilled reality."

Hertzel was right. It took forty-four years from the day of his death for the State of Israel to come into being. If you care to trace it, you will see, step-by-step, how God's two people are being restored—Israel, politically and nationally, and the church, spiritually.

God also showed me the cause of the desolation. One day, I was meditating on the condition of the church, thinking particularly of the response I had received to certain kinds of messages I had delivered. For instance, when I would preach on the need for forgiveness, at least half the Christians in the room would stand up to acknowledge that there was someone they needed to forgive. In some of the large congregations where I had preached on deliverance, three out of four people indicated that they needed deliverance. Commonly, I would get a response of two hundred people out of six hundred. And I thought to myself, *Is this the real picture of the church? Is this how things really are? Could it be like that?*

BACK TO OUR INHERITANCE

As I was meditating on these experiences, God spoke to me very clearly in my mind, saying, *You have preached about Joel, beginning with desolation. Did you ever stop to think what caused the desolation?* In my thoughts, I responded, *No, but I get it now—an invading army of insects.* I had read it for myself in the second chapter of Joel: *"the locust…the cankerworm, and the caterpiller, and the palmerworm"* (Joel 2:25 KJV). In that passage, God calls them *"my great army"* (verse 25 KJV). Then the Lord spoke to me again very clearly in my mind: *My people have been systematically infiltrated by the forces of the enemy.*

That is unquestionably the truth. Once you have seen the evidence, it is as apparent as can be. The church of Jesus Christ has been systematically invaded and infiltrated by invading armies of evil spirits, and they are entrenched. But when the Holy Spirit comes, they will have to leave. I thank God that they are on their way out—not happily, not willingly, but they are going.

Then God gave me an additional insight: *You can see how far away My people Israel have been for eighteen centuries from their God-given inheritance.* I knew immediately that this was obvious. I knew enough history to realize that the Jews had been exiles, wandering away from Israel and their God-given inheritance in that land, for more than eighteen centuries. The Lord said to me, *In My sight, the church has been just as far away from its spiritual inheritance as Israel has been from their political inheritance.*

We all know the tremendous distance Israel has had to go to get her land back. The church has a similar journey to make. Israel did not get back her inheritance without struggle, sacrifice, and conflict. Neither will the church. It will take a battle.

THE CHURCH'S ROLE IN RESTORATION

In light of the role the church is to play in the days ahead, I want to suggest that the key word in relation to the present move of the Holy Spirit is *restoration*. The church has had a reformation. It can no longer have merely a reformation. There is only one goal that will qualify now—*restoration*. No longer will it suffice for the church to improve and patch up man's methods and systems. Now we must have God restoring His divine pattern, purpose, and order—that is the only action God is interested in.

This observation may shock you, but it is my firm opinion that God is not interested in reviving any denomination. I say this not to be in any sense negative or critical but simply to state a fact. People who are seeking to use the outpouring of the Holy Spirit for their own denominational ends are going to miss the purpose of God entirely. He is restoring the body of Jesus Christ. He is gathering together His scattered sheep from all lands and nations, and He has declared that at the end of this age there will be one flock and one Shepherd. (See John 10:16.) That is the purpose of God.

In Genesis, we read, "*...and unto him* [the Messiah] *shall the gathering of the people be*" (Genesis 49:10 KJV). We are not going to gather around a human leader, a human setup, or a human organization. We are gathering around one

Person, the Head of the church, the Lord Jesus Christ. This is the purpose of God—*restoration*.

We have seen that the Lord Jesus Christ has left us with the authority and the responsibility to be the executors of His purposes on earth. We are not to sit passively on the sidelines and say, "Well, God is going to do it." We are to be intimately involved with His purposes. Jesus taught us to become identified with God's kingdom when He said, in the Lord's Prayer, *"Your kingdom come"* (Matthew 6:10). Then He gave us the reason we are here—to be intimately involved with the business of the kingdom: *"Your will be done on earth as it is in heaven"* (verse 10).

ISRAEL DID NOT GET BACK HER INHERITANCE WITHOUT STRUGGLE, SACRIFICE, AND CONFLICT. NEITHER WILL THE CHURCH.

Do you believe that God's will can be done as perfectly on earth as it is in heaven? Apparently it can, for Jesus said we could pray for it to be so. But, my dear friend, it is not going to happen without you and me. We are implicated. The responsibility is ours. *"Your kingdom come. Your will be done on earth* [in me] *as it is in heaven."*

Do you want to be identified with God's kingdom and the outworking of His will on the earth? Why not let the Lord know this? You can do so by using the following simple prayer:

Lord, I want to be an ambassador for You. I want to be an agent of reconciliation in the earth. With Your help, I will join with Your people in Your work, bringing restoration in the place of desolation. Lord, please help me to that end. Amen.

CHAPTER 15

THE WEAPON OF "MASS RESTORATION"

In connection with the theme of restoration that we discussed in the previous chapter, I want to focus now on a subject that very seldom produces "Hallelujah's" or even "Amen's" from believers. Why? Because in this chapter we will be learning about the role of fasting as a major means of restoration that God has made available to His people.

By fasting, I mean deliberately abstaining from food for spiritual purposes for a certain period of time. I would say that, normally, fasting does not mean you abstain from drink, although this is sometimes the case. Moses twice went without food or drink for forty days. So did Elijah. That type of fasting is supernatural, and I would not recommend it. I would never recommend that you go beyond seventy-two hours without fluids. That is my personal opinion. I know a brother in the Lord who fasted for seventeen days without food or water. However, unless you are going to move out into a supernatural realm, I would not advise that. Luke 4:2 tells us that Jesus fasted for forty days, *"and afterward, when they had ended, He was hungry."* It does not say He was thirsty. The implication is that He did not go without liquids but without food.

I have friends who have done a forty-day fast (with liquids), so it is perfectly possible. But I would not suggest that you start thinking in terms of that length of fast. Set a small objective for yourself and then achieve it. That will be much more satisfying than setting a big objective for yourself and failing to achieve it. Even to go without two meals can be very, very effective. The main issue about fasting, as with other disciplines we practice for God, is our motive. You can fast for forty days for the wrong motives and end up with no results except for feeling miserable and being somewhat thinner.

GOD'S CHOSEN FAST

In the Scriptures, we find a powerful revelation of the fast that God has chosen:

Is this not the fast that I have chosen: To loose the bonds of wickedness, to undo the heavy burdens, to let the oppressed go free, and that you break every yoke? Is it not to share your bread with the hungry, and that you bring to your house the poor who are cast out; when you see the naked, that you cover him, and not hide yourself from your own flesh? Then your light shall break forth like the morning, your healing shall spring forth speedily, and your righteousness shall go before you; the glory of the LORD shall be your rear guard. Then you shall call, and the LORD will answer; you shall cry, and He will say, "Here I am." If you take away the yoke from your midst, the pointing of the finger, and speaking wickedness, if you extend your soul to the hungry and satisfy the afflicted soul, then your light shall dawn in the darkness, and your darkness shall be as the noonday. The LORD will guide you continually, and satisfy your soul in drought, and strengthen your bones; you shall be like a watered garden, and like a spring of water, whose waters do not fail. Those from among you shall build the old waste places; you shall raise up the foundations of many generations; and you shall be called the Repairer of the Breach, The Restorer of Streets to Dwell In.

(Isaiah 58:6–12)

First of all, let me point out that in the first five verses of Isaiah 58, God set aside a certain pattern of fasting as being totally ineffective. It is fasting in which the motives are wrong and the relationships of the people involved are wrong. It is *"for strife and debate, and to strike with the fist of wickedness"* (Isaiah 58:4). It is a mere outward religious ritual, such as a man bowing his head like a bulrush and going through certain motions. God says, "If you want to make your voice heard on high, that is not the way to fast."

If you are familiar with the Orthodox Jews, the above is a vivid picture of the way they pray. I say this is in no sense to criticize the Orthodox Jews, but it is a fact that they will sit and repeat prayers in Hebrew for hours. Many of them do not actually understand the words. But as they repeat these prayers, their heads bow to and fro without ceasing, just like bulrushes bobbing to and fro in the wind.

In the above passage, God was saying, "As far as getting My ear in heaven is concerned, that type of fasting is out. Your relationships are wrong; your motives are wrong. It is just an external ordinance, a tradition you have been rooted in. But it will not get you anywhere with Me."

Then God began to speak about the motive and the purpose for the fast that is acceptable to Him. Frankly, when I read the promises that follow, it makes me think, *I want to get in on this.* Let's examine some of these promises together.

> *Then* [if you fast in the recommended way] *your light shall break forth like the morning, your healing shall spring forth speedily, and your righteousness shall go before you; the glory of the LORD shall be your rear guard. Then you shall call, and the LORD will answer; you shall cry, and He will say, "Here I am." If you take away the yoke from your midst, the pointing of the finger, and speaking wickedness….*
>
> (Isaiah 58:8–9)

What will occur? You will have God close at hand—what more could you want?

> *The LORD will guide you continually, and satisfy your soul in drought, and strengthen your bones* [Do you want to be guided continually? This is one of the secrets.]*; you shall be like a watered garden, and like a spring of water, whose waters do not fail.* [Drought will be all

around you, but you will have the fountains springing up inside.]

(Isaiah 58:11)

After Isaiah shared all these powerful promises related to the fast that God has chosen, he came to the key thought:

Those from among you shall build the old waste places; you shall raise up the foundations of many generations; and you shall be called the Repairer of the Breach, the Restorer of Streets to Dwell In.

(Isaiah 58:12)

Please notice that the one who engages in the fast God has chosen will be the one to bring restoration. That person will repair the breach and rebuild the defenses that have been broken down around God's vineyard.

STANDING IN THE GAP

In Ezekiel 22:30–31, God said this concerning His people Israel at a certain time:

So I sought for a man among them who would make a wall, and stand in the gap before Me on behalf of the land, that I should not destroy it; but I found no one. Therefore I have poured out My indignation on them.

What God was saying here is very clear: "If I could have found one man, I could have turned away My wrath. Just one man who would stand in the hedge, make up the gap, be a repairer of the breach. But I could not find one."

However, as we just read in Isaiah 58, God says in His Word that there *is* a way in which you can become a repairer of the breach, a restorer of streets to dwell in. You can raise up the foundations of many generations; you can restore the old waste places.

When you look at the church of Jesus Christ, it is just as desolate as the land of Israel has been. It is full of old waste places, the ruins of many generations. The people in Nehemiah's day must have asked about the broken-down city of Jerusalem, "Can all this rubble and all this mess ever be built up into a city again?" Similarly, we ask, "Can these ruins of the church be restored?" We find our answer in Isaiah 58:12, directed to the one who fasts according to God's instructions: *"You shall raise up the foundations of many generations; and you shall be called the Repairer of the Breach, the Restorer of Streets to Dwell In."*

YOU CAN RAISE UP THE FOUNDATIONS OF MANY GENERATIONS; YOU CAN RESTORE THE OLD WASTE PLACES.

It is my personal conviction that, without exception, every man whose ministry has made an impact that stretches through generations has been a man of fasting and prayer. It is not possible within the scope of this book to go through a comprehensive list of such men, but I would like to mention two noteworthy people.

JOHN WESLEY

The early Methodists were people of fasting and prayer. They took it for granted that their congregations would fast. Wesley stated explicitly that he would not ordain a man to the Methodist ministry who would not undertake to fast twice a week, Wednesday and Friday, until four o'clock in the afternoon.

I am not saying that fasting is the only discipline we need. However, I am pointing out that wherever God's people have known real power, one of the secrets of that power has been their fasting.

CHARLES FINNEY

Finney went out into the forest and received a glorious experience of conversion and the baptism of the Holy Spirit. In that moment, he was endowed with supernatural power.

In Finney's ministry, conviction fell wherever he went, and sinners turned to God. He says in his own autobiography, "At times I would find myself comparatively empty of this power. I would go out in the woods and spend a day or two in fasting and prayer. The power returned and I was able to move back in my ministry."

MY EXPERIENCE OF FASTING

Some people regard fasting as a kind of awful specter held in front of them. As far as I am concerned, I am so grateful to God that I discovered this way to get through to Him. The Holy Spirit taught me a lesson about fasting immediately after I was saved and baptized in the Holy Spirit. I was a soldier in the British Army in the North African desert. I didn't have a church. I didn't have a man near me who knew the Lord, and I didn't have a minister to go to. I had the Bible and the Holy Spirit. Without planning it, I also began to fast regularly on Wednesday of every week.

In that part of the world, which is primarily Muslim, those who practice Islam have a month in the year that they call Ramadan. During that time, they do not eat in the daytime. No orthodox Muslim will eat from dawn to sunset, nor will their beasts drink, throughout the month of Ramadan. I lived in a strict Muslim area in the Sudan, and I noticed that they would not touch a drop of water, even though the temperature was often well over a hundred. The British soldiers, knowing this, used to call Wednesday "Ramadan," because they knew I would not eat on that day. I did not do this to be seen in front of the other soldiers. But when you live in a truck in the desert with eight people, and you do everything together—sleep together, eat together, and all the rest—it becomes conspicuous if you are not eating.

Now, I do not want to give the impression that fasting will enable you to obtain anything that is outside of the will of God for you. It won't. If something is outside of God's will, there is no God-given way of getting it. For instance, as a result of an adulterous relationship, King David had a son, and that son was smitten; he was sickly and dying. David fasted for a week, yet the son died. God had said the son would die, and David could not change God's judgment or His word by fasting. So, if you want something that is wrong or outside of God's will, fasting will not get it for you.

But there is another side to this. There are outcomes within the will of God that we will never attain without fasting. They are there, and God offers them to us—but the only way into them is by fasting and prayer. In particular, I believe that wherever God's people have distanced themselves from their inheritance, one essential step back to that inheritance is fasting.

CHAPTER 16

HISTORY CHANGERS

As we continue in this chapter to examine the power of fasting as a spiritual weapon God has placed in the hands of His people, I would like to illustrate this truth with several vivid examples from the Old Testament. But first, let us examine the last verse of the book of 1 Samuel. This Scripture is speaking of the men of Jabesh Gilead:

> *Then they took their bones* [the bones of Saul and his sons, who had been slain in battle by the Philistines] *and buried them under the tamarisk tree at Jabesh, and fasted seven days.* (1 Samuel 31:13)

A SEVEN-DAY LESSON

I mentioned previously that in the early 1950s, we had a mission work in London, England. God showed me that for the sake of our work, I needed to fast. So, in November, I embarked on a seven-day fast. As you may guess, England in November is a pretty chilly, dank place. I remember that about halfway through this seven-day fast, my toes were cold, my fingers were cold, and I felt just plain miserable. In fact, I really wondered at the time if I was going to die.

I thought to myself, *Maybe I've overdone it. Maybe this is fanaticism....* And the devil was right there encouraging these doubts in my mind. (The devil loves to warn us against fanaticism.) My Bible was open in front of me, and just as I was struggling with these thoughts, my eyes fell on this verse about the men of Jabesh Gilead who *"fasted seven days"* (1 Samuel 31:13). Instantly, something like heaven's electricity surged spontaneously through my body, from the crown of my head to the soles of my feet, and I said, "If they could do it, so can I." I declared that I could—and I did. And so can you. (Unless you have a physical limitation, you can fast, also—not that I am telling you to do it. Let God lead you.)

WHEN GOD'S PEOPLE SEEK HIM SERIOUSLY IN FASTING, THE COURSE OF HISTORY IS ALWAYS ALTERED.

But it didn't end there. The Lord led me to examine this passage further. He showed me that I should consider the difference between the course of events in 1 Samuel and the course of events in 2 Samuel. I did, and it is most startling.

First Samuel has a downward bent. It speaks of disobedience, defeat, division, and disaster—that is the summary of 1 Samuel.

By the end of the book, Israel was in the most desperate situation it had ever faced. Their anointed king had been killed, his sons had been killed, their armies had been defeated in battle, they were refugees (many had fled to the east side of the Jordan), and the Philistines had invaded the land and practically taken it over. Furthermore, Ziklag, the particular city where King David lived, had been invaded and burned by the Amalekites while he was away. All of David's family members and possessions had been taken. He was left without any possessions whatsoever. Never had Israel been in such a critical position.

In contrast, 2 Samuel is a book of restoration, reunification, victory, and conquest. It describes conditions that are the exact opposite of the circumstances recorded in 1 Samuel. The whole downward process was reversed and changed, and the transformation came between the two books. So, the Lord said to me, *You have the explanation in the last verse of the first book—the men of Jabesh Gilead* ***"fasted seven days."*** That is what changed the course of events. When God's people become earnest enough to seek Him seriously in fasting, the course of history is always altered.

God's people are here to change history. If we are not doing that, we are failing God. We are the salt of the earth. We are here to have an influence in the world—a unique influence. Jesus said that if we are not doing so, we are like salt that has lost its flavor. We are then *"good for nothing but to be thrown out and trampled underfoot by men"* (Matthew 5:13).

That means you and me. If we are not history changers—if we do not exercise a vital influence in our community, in our city, in our nation, and in the world—we are salt that has lost its flavor. As I have said, I believe that the men whose feet will trample upon us are not far away. There are about a billion of them ready and waiting to do it.

DIVINE INSTRUMENTS OF RESTORATION

DANIEL

We now continue our examination of the pivotal role fasting plays in the outcomes of world history. We will look at several biblical characters, beginning with the life of Daniel. Please bear in mind that what we are studying in this chapter is in the context of key figures in Scripture who were divine instruments of restoration. As I pointed out earlier, every single one of these people practiced fasting.

One of the greatest disasters that came upon God's people Israel was the Babylonian-Persian captivity. During this period of captivity, the man who set the process of restoration in motion spiritually was Daniel. In the ninth chapter of the book of Daniel, we read these words:

In the first year of Darius the son of Ahasuerus, of the lineage of the Medes, who was made king over the realm of the Chaldeans; in the first year of his reign I, Daniel, understood by the books the number of the years specified by the word of the LORD through Jeremiah the prophet, that He would accomplish seventy years in the desolations of Jerusalem.
(Daniel 9:1–2)

Through studying the writings of Jeremiah in the Scriptures, Daniel understood that the desolations of Jerusalem were to last seventy years. He knew enough to understand that the time was nearly finished. So, what did he do? Did he sit back and say, "Now, isn't that wonderful? We are soon going to be restored"? No. He identified himself with God's purpose.

A REVELATION OF GOD'S PLAN IS NOT AN EXCUSE FOR US TO DO NOTHING. IT IS A CHALLENGE FOR US TO PARTICIPATE.

We need to understand that a revelation of God's plan is not an excuse for us to do nothing. It is a challenge for us to participate. Daniel took it that way. He said, in effect, "Now I know what to give myself to in prayer—the fulfillment of this divine purpose."

Daniel saw clearly that he was involved in the accomplishment of God's purpose. He had something to do with the coming of God's kingdom. He was to be an instrument by which God's will could be done as perfectly on earth as it was to be done in heaven.

> Then I set my face toward the Lord God to make request by prayer and supplications, with fasting, sackcloth, and ashes. And I prayed to the Lord my God…. (Daniel 9:3–4)

In the twenty-third verse of that chapter, Daniel's answer came. We will not cover the process in detail in this section. However, without question, it was the prayer and fasting of Daniel that was the spiritual instrument God used to set in motion the restoration of Israel from captivity.

The same principle is true for you and me, dear friend. When we see in God's Word that He is going to move, to restore, to pour out His Spirit, we do not sit back and say, "Isn't that wonderful?" We say, "Here is the purpose I am to become identified with. Here is what I am to give myself to in prayer and fasting and by every other means God puts at my disposal. I am to become identified with God's business." That is how we get involved in God's process of restoration.

EZRA

Proceeding to the next great biblical figure of restoration, we turn to the book of Ezra. In the eighth chapter, we find a very interesting situation. Ezra had been appointed by the king of Persia to lead a host of returning exiles to take back to Jerusalem all the sacred vessels belonging to the temple of the Lord. They were transporting unique articles of gold and silver of tremendous value.

So here was Ezra with the returning company of exiles—men, women, and children—and he had in his possession the most fantastically precious vessels of gold and silver. His assignment was to take a long journey through rugged country where there were bandits and armed robbers and marauders. How was he to get through safely? What means was he to use? You can see that Ezra was confronted with a choice. He could use spiritual means or he could use carnal means. His decision is recorded in Ezra 8:

> *Then I proclaimed a fast there at the river of Ahava, that we might humble ourselves before our God, to seek from Him the right way for us and our little ones and all our possessions. For I was ashamed to request of the king an escort of soldiers and horsemen to help us against the enemy on the road, because we had spoken to the king, saying, "The hand of our God is upon all those for good who seek Him, but His power and His wrath are against all those who forsake Him." So we fasted and entreated our God for this, and He answered our prayer.*
> (Ezra 8:21–23)

In verse 31, we find the historical fulfillment of their mission:

> *Then we departed from the river of Ahava on the twelfth day of the first month, to go to Jerusalem. And the hand of our God was upon us, and He delivered us from the hand of the enemy and from ambush along the road.*
> (Ezra 8:31)

Notice that there were plenty of enemies and plenty of people lying in wait. But the people of Israel were delivered from them. Why? Because they got the victory in the spiritual realm before they started the journey. Again, Ezra had the choice between two means. He could have asked the king for a band of soldiers and horsemen to give them a safe escort. However, Ezra had put himself on the spot by his testimony, and this is one of the benefits of testifying. When you testify, you have to live up to it.

THE PEOPLE WHO KNOW HOW TO INTERVENE IN THE SPIRITUAL REALM BECOME THE KEY FACTOR IN HUMAN AFFAIRS.

Ezra had told the king, "We have a God who looks after His servants. He protects us; He watches over us; He keeps us. He possesses all power. He is not just the God of the land of Israel or the God of the land of Egypt. He is the God of all lands and all nations. They are all in His hand—they are all under His control."

So, when the king said, "Take this group of people back to Jerusalem," Ezra realized he could not then go to the king and say, "Would you please give us a band of soldiers and horsemen?" By his own testimony, he had limited himself to the spiritual means to fulfill his mission. What were those means? *"We fasted and entreated our God"* (Ezra 8:23).

I want to remind you of something very significant: When you get the victory in the spiritual realm, you have the victory—period. That is all that is needed. The spiritual victory is the decisive element in all matters. The people who know how to intervene in the spiritual realm become the key factor in human affairs. That is why the members of the body of Christ should be the decisive factor—they alone have the means. *"For the weapons of our warfare are not carnal but mighty in God for pulling down strongholds"* (2 Corinthians 10:4). That is what God has put us here for.

I would also say this, just as my testimony: I would never make a major move or any major commitment without fasting and prayer. I would be scared to do it. Lydia and I traveled from land to land and continent to continent and took our little ones with us. I can testify that the God of Ezra is my God. He has not changed. Seek Him in fasting and prayer. He will watch over you. He will make a way. He will protect you and your little ones. It is wonderful.

NEHEMIAH

Another great figure in the restoration process is Nehemiah. What did Nehemiah do when he heard about the situation of the broken-down wall and burned gates of the city of Jerusalem?

> *So it was, when I heard these words, that I sat down and wept, and mourned for many days; I was fasting and praying before the God of heaven.*
>
> (Nehemiah 1:4)

We will not go into Nehemiah's entire story here. Rather, I simply present his confirmation of the place of fasting and prayer in the process of restoration.

ESTHER

Next is one of the most outstanding examples of the truth of the power of fasting. It comes from the story of Esther, who, along with many other Jews, lived under the rule of the Persian Empire during the captivity. Please note that this story is also a demonstration of the process of restoration.

In the days of Esther, there lived a certain man named Haman, who is a type of Satan, the adversary of God's people. This evil man procured from the great emperor of Persia an edict by which all the Jews in every province of the kingdom were to be destroyed on a specific day.

Incidentally, all through this story, there is a conflict of spirits. For example, if you study the behavior of Haman, you will find that he cast lots to determine the right day for the massacre to take place. In other words, he was seeking guidance from his deities—spirits in the unseen realm—to get them on his side so he might find the best time to destroy the Israelites. Actually, Haman came nearer to this goal than Adolf Hitler did, because he managed to obtain an actual decree that all the Jews in the 127 provinces of Persia were to be destroyed on a certain day. Simply stated, once a decree was made by the king of Persia, it could not be undone.

Mordecai, a Jewish leader who was present daily in the king's citadel, heard the decree, went out into the streets, and put on sackcloth, which was a sign of fasting and mourning. Esther the queen was Mordecai's cousin; moreover, she had been raised by him after her parents died. She sent him garments and offered to clothe him. Mordecai said, in effect, "Don't offer me your clothing. I want to stay in sackcloth." Then Esther sent a message to him to inquire what the trouble was, and his reply was essentially this: "Esther, you are in a unique position. You have the ear of the king. You can go to him and procure an edict that will change the destiny of your people."

Esther sent another message to Mordecai, saying, "But you know the law. Any person who goes into the king's presence without being summoned is risking a sentence of death, unless the king stretches out the golden scepter." Mordecai replied, "You have no alternative. That is what you are here for." In response, Esther said, "All right. If I perish, I perish. I am in this thing to live or die." Esther's attitude was like that of the believers mentioned in Revelation 12:11: "*…and they did not love their lives to the death.*" That is the kind of people God is looking for. People who are committed to Him, who believe that whether they live or die is not important.

Esther said to Mordecai, "Go and gather all the Jews who are in Shushan and fast for me. Neither eat nor drink for three days, day and night, and I and my maidens will do likewise. Then I will go in to see the king." (See Esther 4.)

On the fourth day, Esther did not put on sackcloth. One reason is that no one could enter into the king's presence clothed in sackcloth. But even more important, it indicated that Esther already had the victory before she went in. She put on her beautiful garments and went in as a queen. When the king saw her, his heart was moved toward her. He stretched out the golden scepter and said, "What do you wish, Queen Esther? What is your petition? It shall be given to you." (See Esther 5:6.)

Esther is one of the great types of the church of Jesus Christ, and a type for our day—in stark contrast to what you find in the first chapter of the book of Esther. There you will discover that previously there had been another queen, named Vashti. Very much like the contemporary, institutional church, Vashti had her own agenda. When the king had sent for her, so that he could show off her beauty to the guests at his feast, Vashti had turned down his invitation and said, "I have my own banquet." (See Esther 1:9–12.)

Isn't that just like the church? "Don't interrupt, Lord. Don't interfere. Just keep Your Holy Spirit away from us. We have our own program." When Vashti refused to come, the king became extremely angry and pronounced a judgment that this queen was never again to appear in his presence.

GOD IS LOOKING FOR PEOPLE WHO ARE COMMITTED TO HIM, WHO BELIEVE THAT WHETHER THEY LIVE OR DIE IS NOT IMPORTANT.

As a result of Vashti's banishment, Esther had become queen. She had gone through a process of preparation—six months with oil of myrrh and six months with perfumes and beauty treatments. Similarly, there will be a process of preparation for the true bride of Jesus Christ. Some of it will be with myrrh (representing bitter circumstances), and some of it will be with sweet spices. But Esther was absolutely obedient to Hegai, the king's eunuch, who is a type of the Holy Spirit. She asked nothing but what Hegai gave. She wanted no extra adornments, no extra carnal attractions, no human agenda. She went in to the king just the way Hegai had prepared her. She was equipped, and she became the queen.

That is what is happening today. God has rejected Vashti, and He is looking for Esther. But I want to emphasize something that is absolutely relevant to you and me. For the appointed person, such as the queen, the position comes with great responsibility. You are the one who can intervene. You are the one who can change history. You are the one who can alter the destiny of a nation.

This reality applies both to individual believers and to the church as a whole. The true church is going to be marked by her interventions in history. And those interventions will originate in fasting and prayer. If you want the position and the privileges, then you must accept the responsibilities that go with them. Citizens of countries whose form of government is a constitutional monarchy clearly understand this principle in relation to royalty—with the position and the privileges also comes the responsibility. You do not qualify if you are not prepared to accept the responsibility.

JOEL

For our final example, let us look to the book of Joel. I mentioned earlier that Joel is the prophet of this latter-day outpouring, this great restoration. Even so, Joel demanded the cooperation of God's people. Three times, the prophet called for fasting and prayer. First, Joel said, "Consecrate a fast, call a sacred assembly" (Joel 1:14). Second, he declared, "Now, therefore," says the LORD, "turn to Me with all your heart, with fasting, with weeping, and with mourning" (Joel 2:12). Finally, he said, "Consecrate a fast, call a sacred assembly; gather the people, sanctify the congregation, assemble the elders" (Joel 2:15–16).

It would have been totally illogical for Joel to give us the preview of the outpouring but then to prescribe out-of-date methods. That would be absurd. Joel showed us what God is going to do, and he showed us how we are to cooperate with God. The part to be played by God's people is to seek Him with fasting and prayer, to "rend our hearts and not our garments" (see Joel 2:13), and to call a sacred assembly.

I would point out to you that the leaders of God's people have a special responsibility. If you are a leader in the church, in any capacity—minister, elder, or lay leader—you are included in that responsibility. It goes with the position. You are to set a pattern for God's people.

In Joel 2:32, we find these words: *"And it shall come to pass...."* God has shown us His plan as clearly in Joel as He showed His plan to Daniel through the writings of Jeremiah. The responsibility that fell upon Daniel now rests upon you and me. This is God's way.

GOD COUNTS ON US
TO BRING ABOUT RESTORATION

Ezekiel 36 is the great restoration chapter for Israel, and it is being fulfilled before our eyes today. Having promised this wonderful restoration, notice what God said:

> *I will also let the house of Israel inquire of Me to do this for them: I will increase their men like a flock.* (Ezekiel 36:37)

He has promised to do it. Yet He says, in effect, "I won't fulfill it completely until they ask Me in prayer."

The same is precisely true of the outpouring of the Holy Spirit. God has shown enough for us to know that He is in the outpouring business. But to see it through to completion, we have to cooperate. (I thank God that so many of His saints are indeed cooperating with His plans and purposes.)

We must recognize that we are important. We are vital. God reckons on us. You may talk about your faith in God, and that is wonderful and true. Yet stop for one moment and think about the faith that God has in you. The thought will humble you. God counts on you and me. Let's not fail Him.

CHAPTER 17

WHEN, NOT IF

In the previous chapter, we focused on the power and impact of fasting by looking at some Old Testament events. We examined the lives of people involved in those events through whom the practice of fasting played a critical, history-changing role.

Some people have criticized me, saying that I preach only from the Old Testament. Therefore, to show you that fasting is plainly practiced in the New Testament, we will begin by looking at the sixth chapter of Matthew. This passage is part of the Sermon on the Mount, which almost everyone agrees is the "charter" for all Christians. As I said at the very beginning of this book, the Sermon on the Mount is our pattern for Christian living.

JESUS EXPECTS US TO FAST

In Matthew 6, Jesus used the word *"when"* about three things: *"...when you do a charitable deed"* (verse 3), *"...when you pray"* (verse 6), and *"...when you fast"* (verse 17). Let's look at each of these practices in more detail.

> But when you do a charitable deed, do not let your left hand know what your right hand is doing. (Matthew 6:3)

But you, when you pray, go into your room, and when you have shut your door, pray to your Father who is in the secret place; and your Father who sees in secret will reward you openly. (Matthew 6:6)

But you, when you fast, anoint your head and wash your face, so that you do not appear to men to be fasting.... (Matthew 6:17–18)

Having been a teacher of the English language, I know that there is a difference between the word *when* and the word *if.* If Jesus had said, "*If you do a charitable deed...,*" "*If you pray...,*" or "*If you fast...,*" He would have left it open as to whether He expected us to do it or not. But by using the word *when,* He settled the question.

Do you believe it is scriptural for Christians to do charitable deeds? Do you believe it is scriptural for Christians to pray? Then it is just as scriptural for Christians to fast. Exactly the same language is used in connection with all three practices.

FASTING GENERATES POWER. IT IS JUST A QUESTION OF WHAT KIND OF POWER IT GENERATES.

We see a similar emphasis in Mark 2, where Jesus is questioned about fasting. Verse 18 tells us, "*The disciples of John and of the Pharisees were fasting.*"

Let me pause here to make an important observation. This verse refers to the disciples of John the Baptist and of the Pharisees. Fasting has always been practiced by earnest religious people, and it still is today—by Buddhists, Muslims, and many others. I would simply observe, as well, that the religions that practice fasting have more power than the non-fasting religions. If we want to have more power than the religions that are opposed to Christianity, we cannot accomplish this aim without fasting.

When I lived in a purely Muslim land during the month of Ramadan, it sometimes felt as if the heavens were covered over with clouds of darkness. It was as if hell were just a step away. Do you know what generated that oppressive power? The fasting of the Muslims.

Fasting generates power. It is just a question of what kind of power it generates. If you do not know anything about Islam and Muslims, you might misunderstand me. But even so, let me tell you clearly—and I'm not seeking to offend anybody—that the god of Islam is the devil. That does not mean God does not love Muslims. But it is a hellish system.

A MARK OF DISCIPLESHIP

Returning now to our text in Mark 2, we read:

The disciples of John and of the Pharisees were fasting. Then they came and said to Him [Jesus], "Why do the disciples of John and of the Pharisees fast, but Your disciples do not fast?" And Jesus said to them, "Can the friends of the bridegroom fast while the bridegroom is with them? As long as they have the bridegroom with them they cannot fast. But the days will come when the bridegroom will be taken away from them, and then they will fast in those days." (Mark 2:18–20)

Jesus answered the question with a little parable, and I will give you my interpretation of it. When He talked about the bridegroom, He was talking about Himself. When He talked about the friends of the bridegroom, He was talking about His disciples. He was saying, "While the Bridegroom is with the friends of the Bridegroom, they cannot fast. So, don't expect them to fast while I am personally present upon the earth. But the days will come when the Bridegroom will be taken away from them. And in those days they will fast."

As I understand this passage and how it applies to us today, the personal presence of Jesus the Bridegroom has been taken away from us. We are awaiting His return. That means He is not here now. Clearly, Jesus said, "In those days, the friends of the Bridegroom, the disciples of Christ, *will* fast."

What is one mark of discipleship? Fasting. Frankly, if you do not do it, you lack one of the God-appointed marks of a disciple of Jesus Christ.

FASTING IN THE EARLY CHURCH

The believers of the early church fasted frequently and publicly. In the thirteenth chapter of the book of Acts, we read the following account:

> *Now in the church that was at Antioch there were certain prophets and teachers: Barnabas, Simeon…, Lucius…, Manaen…, and Saul. As they ministered to the Lord and fasted, the Holy Spirit said, "Now separate to Me Barnabas and Saul for the work to which I have called them."*
>
> (Acts 13:1–2)

The leading ministers of that local congregation in Antioch came together collectively and sought God in prayer and fasting. As a result, they received a special divine revelation. The first actual missionary project we read about in the New Testament was an answer to the fasting and prayer of the leaders of the early church. "Separate to Me Barnabas and Saul. I have a special job for them."

Please notice that when they had this revelation, they did not immediately act on it, as indicated in the following verse:

> *Then, having fasted and prayed, and laid hands on them, they sent them away.*
>
> (Acts 13:3)

WE SHOULD PRAY THROUGH AND FAST THROUGH IN ORDER TO OBTAIN THE VICTORY.

Again they fasted and prayed. The first time they fasted, they received the revelation. The second time they fasted, they obtained the victory before they sent Barnabas and Saul out. That is how it should be in mission work. That is how it should be in the Lord's work. We should have the victory before we go out. We should pray through and fast through in order to obtain the victory.

My family was on the mission field in East Africa for five years. During that time, Lydia and I practiced fasting regularly, every Thursday. (Mind you, I am not in any sense boasting.

But if I never practiced fasting myself, I certainly could not preach it to others.)

In East Africa, I had been appointed principal of a college, and I was very busy during those years—from 6:00 AM to 10:00 PM, every day, Sunday included. At first, I decided I was too busy to fast. But after a little while, I found that my spiritual life was not what it ought to have been. In the beginning, I could not put my finger on any specific cause. Then I realized, *I had better not be too busy to fast.*

As a matter of fact, in his journals, John Wesley said that if a person once receives the light on fasting and fails to practice it, he will backslide as surely as a person who has the light on prayer and fails to pray. I can bear witness to Wesley's statement—he is right.

So, I went back to my fasting. By the time I left East Africa, I had made many mistakes. But basically I knew I had accomplished the work for which God had sent me there. I give much of the credit to the practice of fasting.

CONVINCING RESULTS

Continuing with the account of Paul and Barnabas, when they returned from their journey, they gave a report of the work they had accomplished. (See Acts 14:27.) To put it simply, they got the job done. When I was in East Africa, God revealed a truth to me in the form of a sentence: *If you want New Testament results, you have to use New Testament methods; there is no other way.*

In the fourteenth chapter of Acts, we find further confirmation concerning the practice of fasting in the early church:

> *So when they* [Paul and Barnabas] *had appointed elders in every church, and prayed with fasting, they commended them to the Lord in whom they had believed.* (Acts 14:23)

Notice that in every church, they prayed with fasting. This was not just the practice in one church. It was a regular practice in every church under the leadership of the apostles. And so it should be today.

Paul said that in all things, he commended himself as a minister of God: *"in much patience, in tribulations, in needs, in distresses, in stripes, in imprisonments, in tumults, in labors, in sleeplessness, [and] in fastings"* (2 Corinthians 6:4–5). One way we confirm ourselves as ministers of God is by our fasting.

In 2 Corinthians 11, Paul wrote this about his own personal experience and ministry:

> *…in weariness and toil, in sleeplessness often, in hunger and thirst, in fastings often, in cold and nakedness….*   (2 Corinthians 11:27)

Paul made a distinction between hunger and thirst, and fasting. Hunger and thirst is when you *can't* eat or drink because you don't have any food or water. But fasting is when you deliberately *don't* eat for spiritual purposes. Paul's comment was that he was *"in fastings often."*

FASTING CAN CHANGE THE WORLD

It is possible for us to change history. I am absolutely convinced of this. I am not preaching a theory. I am telling you about something that actually works; it produces results. I sincerely believe God expects us to be history changers. In fact, history *needs* to be changed.

The course of events in the world today desperately needs to be altered. It can be changed—we can do it. History, as recorded in the Scriptures, shows time and again that when God's people have gotten earnest enough to deny their appetites and seek Him, setting aside the material and temporary pursuits of this world, God has moved in response. And history has been changed.

There are also many such records outside of the Bible—times when men and women became desperate, prayed, and sought God, and the whole course of events was altered. There is no doubt that in the Second World War, when the British nation proclaimed the Day of Prayer—at that critical moment—God intervened at Dunkirk. It definitely happened. I have spoken to many men who were eyewitnesses of what took place. When a nation will humble itself before God, there is almost nothing that God will not do. Our pride and our self-sufficiency are the barriers that hold God back.

CAN WE LEARN FROM AHAB?

At this point in our discussion of fasting, let me bring up an unusual but remarkable event described for us in 1 Kings 21. The prophet Elijah was sent to proclaim the judgment of God upon King Ahab and his whole household because of the king's blatant wickedness. The message was that Ahab and his household would be blotted out completely. Yet when Ahab, this wicked king, received the message from God, he turned his face to the wall and sought the Lord with prayer and fasting. And God said, in effect, "Because he has humbled himself, I will spare him and his generation." (See 1 Kings 21:29.)

If God would do that for King Ahab when he prayed and fasted, how much more would He do for you if you would pray and fast? Let's read the actual words that are recorded at the end of 1 Kings 21:

> *But there was no one like Ahab who sold himself to do wickedness in the sight of the* Lord, *because Jezebel his wife stirred him up. And he behaved very abominably in following idols, according to all that the Amorites had done, whom the* Lord *had cast out before the children of Israel.*
> (1 Kings 21:25–26)

There was no one quite so wicked as Ahab. But, as we noted, look what happened due to the king's response to God:

> *So it was, when Ahab heard those words [of God's judgment], that he tore his clothes and put sackcloth on his body, and fasted and lay in sackcloth, and went about mourning. And the word of the* Lord *came to Elijah the Tishbite, saying, "See how Ahab has humbled himself before Me? Because he has humbled himself before Me, I will not bring the calamity in his days. In the days of his son I will bring the calamity on his house."*
> (1 Kings 21:27–29)

Even Ahab could cause the judgment of God to be suspended for one generation when he became earnest enough to seek the Lord with prayer and fasting. Once again, how much more should the results of prayer and fasting apply to you! You are part of a chosen generation. You are one of God's people. If God would do that for a wicked, idolatrous king, what will He do for the church of Jesus Christ when it becomes as earnest as Ahab was? There would never be the great condemnation upon us in the last day if we were willing to become as earnest as King Ahab.

"SEEK MY FACE"

We covered the following Scripture previously, but it is worth examining again. In 2 Chronicles 7:14, God says:

> *...if My people who are called by My name will humble themselves, and pray and seek My face, and turn from their wicked ways, then I will hear from heaven, and will forgive their sin and heal their land.*

You are one of God's people, called by His name. You are a Christian because the name of Christ is called upon you. This wonderful promise in 2 Chronicles is for you, and you can count on it, because:

> *All the promises of God in Him [Christ] are Yes, and in Him Amen, to the glory of God through us.*   (2 Corinthians 1:20)

The promise in 2 Chronicles is included among *"all the promises of God."* You are identified as one of the people of God upon whom Christ's name is called, so this promise is for you. Remember what we covered earlier. God said that if His people who are called by His name will take four actions—humble themselves, pray, seek His face, and turn from their wicked ways—then He promises three responses: He will hear from heaven, He will forgive their sin (whose sin? The sin of His people), and He will heal the land in which they live.

I was trained as a logician, and, to me, there is one clear deduction from 2 Chronicles 7:14. We discussed this conclusion earlier: If the land is not healed, the fault is with the people of God. No matter what country you live in, I believe that the responsibility for the condition of your nation lies at the door of the people of God. It is the church that is responsible—not the corrupt politicians, not the crooked businessmen, not the revolutionaries, but the church.

The church is answerable for the land in which it lives. It always has been. The church is the salt of the earth. But *"if the salt loses its flavor* [if it does not do its job],...*it is then good for nothing"* (Matthew 5:13).

Once more, that is a solemn phrase: *"good for nothing."* But that is what we are if we are not doing our job. And that is what Jesus was saying in the above verse: "You are good for nothing if you are not doing your job as a Christian."

THE HARDEST STEP

Let me emphasize again that the first step required of God's people is not to pray but to humble themselves. That is the hardest step to take, but if you can get religious people to humble themselves, anything can happen. I quoted before what Evan Roberts said in the great Welsh Revival of 1904: "Bend the church and bow the world." It is not hard to bow the world when you can bend the church. It is the stiff-necked, self-righteous, self-sufficient churchgoer who stands between God and revival.

So, God's people are the ones who have to humble themselves. It has always been this way. You can see this truth all through the Bible. For example, it is clearly stated in the first epistle of Peter: *"For the time has come for judgment to begin at the house of God"* (1 Peter 4:17). Judgment begins first with us, the church. Peter was not in any doubt as to whom he meant by *"the house of God."* Where will the ungodly and the sinner be found? The answer to this question is unsettling: in the church.

There is an account in Ezekiel 9 in which God sent six men with slaughter weapons through the city to bring judgment on His people. Where did He tell them to begin? *"Begin at My sanctuary"* (Ezekiel 9:6). And with whom did they begin? *"They began with the elders who were before the temple"* (verse 6). So it will be today when God's judgment comes. It will come on His people, and primarily on the leaders. That principle never changes.

Notice again that our responsibility begins with a hard task: we have to humble ourselves. How do you humble yourself? By all means, don't pray, "God, make me humble." That is not a scriptural prayer. God consistently says, in effect, "You have to humble yourself. Don't ask Me to do it." He can humiliate you, if you require it—but only you can humble yourself. Humility is something that comes from within. It is not imposed from without.

A GOOD KIND OF MISERY

As we saw in the earlier passage, Ahab humbled himself by fasting. In Psalm 35:13, David said, *"I humbled my soul with fasting"* (KJV). In other words, "I subdued this ego in me that demands, 'I want this' and 'I want that.'" Jesus said, *"If anyone desires to come after Me* [what is the first step?], *let him deny himself, and take up his cross daily, and follow Me"* (Luke 9:23).

"Let him deny himself." Fasting is denying your old ego. It is denying its wants. It is saying, "No, there's something more important than you. You just wait for a while. I will attend to you when it suits me. Right now, my spirit is going to be taken up with God."

It is good to know a way to humble yourself, and I can tell you from personal experience that fasting makes you feel like a worm. But that is good, because we are worms! I once heard a friend of mine comment on passages from Isaiah 41, including verse 14: *"Fear not, you worm Jacob."* He said, "God can take the worm and make it a sharp threshing instrument to thresh the mountain." (See Isaiah 41:15.) But first the worm must realize it is a worm.

When you are fasting, and you are feeling like a worm, say, "Praise the Lord, now I realize what I am. I am a worm." Fasting makes me feel miserable, but it is a good kind of misery. We all need to be miserable at times. It is this arrogant, striving, self-sufficient ego of ours that gets in God's way. It needs to be humbled. *"I humbled my soul,"* David said, *"with fasting"* (Psalm 35:13). He suppressed his soul; he told it where it belongs—he refused to allow it to dictate affairs of the kingdom of God.

Speaking of humbling ourselves, let's read this wonderful verse from Hebrews:

> *Furthermore, we have had human fathers who corrected us, and we*
> *paid them respect. Shall we not much more readily be in subjection to*
> *the Father of spirits and live?*   (Hebrews 12:9)

Do you want to live? Then be in subjection to the Father of spirits. Submit your spirit to His Spirit. It is a wonderful feeling. Oh, it is good to get down! Sometimes, I have lain down on the ground just to tell myself where I belong. You will hardly find a man of God in the Bible who had not been on his face before the Lord; not one, practically speaking. Where you belong is where you came from, out of the dust. (See Genesis 2:7.) Just get acquainted with that fact.

BEFORE IT'S TOO LATE

We will now look at a remarkable passage in the book of Lamentations. The sad fact of the lamentations of Jeremiah is that they were written, in a sense, too late. In effect, Jeremiah said, "I can see it all. I can see where we went wrong, but it is too late." As far as his particular epoch was concerned, it *was* too late. The judgment of God had passed over. People had been carried away, little children were dying of starvation, men had been killed in war, mothers were bereaved. The city lamented, the people had been put to an open shame, and there was no way to change the course of events. They had waited until it was too late.

Lamentations is a tragic book. But it is good for us to make up our minds that there will not be a book of lamentations over our own country. It is possible for a time to come when it is too late—there is no question about that. You may often feel that such a moment has come for your nation. Personally, I do not believe that, but I think the time is critical. I am convinced the need is urgent.

In Lamentations 3:22, we read, "*Through the LORD's mercies we are not consumed....*" If ever that sentence was true, it is true today. Let's read that phrase again, as well as several verses that follow:

Through the LORD's mercies we are not consumed, because His compassions fail not. They are new every morning; great is Your faithfulness. "The LORD is my portion," says my soul, "therefore I hope in Him!" The LORD is good to those who wait for Him, to the soul who seeks Him. It is good that one should hope and wait quietly for the salvation of the LORD. It is good for a man to bear the yoke in his youth. Let him sit alone and keep silent, because God has laid it on him; let him put his mouth in the dust; there may yet be hope. (Lamentations 3:22–29)

This portion of the above passage was actually part of my personal testimony: *"It is good for a man to bear the yoke in his youth"* (verse 27). That was my condition when the Lord saved me and baptized me in the Holy Spirit many years ago while I was a soldier in the British Army. I remained a soldier for four and a half more years. At that time, I could not see why I had to stay a soldier when the Lord had saved me, baptized me, and called me. However, later, when I looked back on that period of my life, I came to realize that out of the various forms of education I received, the most valuable was the four and a half years I spent in the army after my conversion.

IT IS GOOD FOR US TO MAKE UP OUR MINDS THAT THERE WILL NOT BE A BOOK OF LAMENTATIONS OVER OUR OWN COUNTRY.

I can remember being in the desert, day after day, night after night, for months on end, never seeing a paved road. I was surrounded by carnal, blaspheming soldiers who had no interest in God or the things of God. I was unable to escape because there was no way I could get away from it. There came moments of desperation when I sat alone and kept silent—and I even put my mouth in the dust, just as Lamentations 3:29 says. You might not think of the literal fulfillment of such a verse. But I remember many times when I cast myself down upon my face on the surface of the desert and put my mouth in the dust, that *"there may yet be hope."* I did not enjoy it, but it was very good for me. That is where we belong—in the dust.

If you will follow the prescription in Joel that we examined earlier, get down on your face in the dust before God, humble yourself, rend your heart and not your garment, seek God with all your heart, and set aside every material distraction, God will rend the heavens and come down. The mountains will melt at His presence, and we will see a mighty Holy Spirit revival. (See Isaiah 64:1.) We are on the winning side!

DO BUSINESS WITH GOD

There is a passage in the book of Micah that says the *"breaker"* has gone up, and the king has gone before his people.

> *The breaker is come up before them: they have broken up, and have passed through the gate, and are gone out by it: and their king shall pass before them, and the LORD on the head of them.* (Micah 2:13 KJV)

The *"breaker"* is Jesus Christ. He has gone up—the way has been opened. All we have to do is follow.

Oh, the gospel is good news! Let me never fail to emphasize that truth. It is not a prescription for sitting still and saying, "I'm sorry, but there is nothing I can do." You *can* do something. You can intervene. You can seek God.

Remember the "powerhouse of prayer" that I presented in three verses?

> *Whatever you bind on earth will be bound in heaven.* (Matthew 18:18)

> *If two of you agree on earth concerning anything that they ask, it will be done....* (Matthew 18:19)

> *Where two or three are gathered together in My [Jesus'] name, I am there in the midst of them.* (Matthew 18:20)

There is nothing left out when you consider those tremendous promises. This is the heart of all power. It is the place of authority, and it is encircled, as I told you earlier, with right relationships.

I want to recommend that you set your face to move in and do business with God. I want to challenge you to respond to what we have covered in this chapter. I made a resolution some time ago that I would not merely teach—that I would no longer be content with a mere religious lecture.

As we close this section, I want to make a very definite, practical, and personal application. When I was training teachers in East Africa, I taught them never to just teach a lesson but always to make an application to challenge their students. I never want to leave Bible instruction in the realm of theory. I desire to get it down into practical action.

You are a Christian, living in your nation, and I believe you are called to be the salt of your particular part of the earth. You are accountable to intervene by spiritual means and change what is wrong in your country—to change rulers, governments, and situations through your commitment to God. One major weapon you have to accomplish this transformation is fasting. So, if you would like to make a commitment to fast on behalf of your nation, please allow me to pray for you.

Father, I thank You for this dear one who has responded with enthusiasm and obedience. It is not going to be easy. There will be tests and struggles. You called us into a realm of conflict, but You promised us the victory.

I pray, Lord, for this dear friend reading these words right now— that You will open a way to make this a reality in his or her life.

I ask You to teach this one out of the Scriptures. Please show this man or woman how to enter into the conflict; how to band together with others in small groups, united in the Spirit; how to press the battle to the gates and bring about the establishment of God's kingdom. In Jesus' name, I pray. Amen.

PART IV

THE AUTHORITY OF THE WORD
AND THE BLOOD

CHAPTER 18

THE POWER OF OUR WITNESS

Let us continue with our emphasis that the church of Jesus Christ is the only agency on earth with the authority to administer the victory Christ has obtained on our behalf. I do not believe this task can be accomplished by an individual. The body of Jesus Christ—collectively—is to demonstrate the victory and the authority of Christ. The third chapter of Ephesians states that this is the purpose of God:

> *To the intent that now the manifold wisdom of God might be made known by the church to the principalities and powers in the heavenly places....*
> (Ephesians 3:10)

God has chosen the church as the collective unit to reveal His manifold, many-sided wisdom. Every child of God is a revelation of one aspect of the wisdom of God. You have a special revelation to give, not only to the world but also to principalities and powers in heavenly places. This special revelation of God's wisdom is manifested as His grace in your life. No one else can give the particular revelation you have to give. Together, we are the composite revelation of the manifold, many-sided wisdom of God.

GLORIOUS POTENTIALITIES

When I refer to the glorious potentialities that lie within the church today, I want to underscore again that the tremendous purposes of God are not going to be fulfilled by some gifted, talented individual. They are the business of the church as a whole. God and all creation have been waiting for the church to realize this truth and to fulfill its calling. (See, for example, Romans 8:18–22.)

Let me suggest that God is calling you to have a new sense of responsibility, not just on an individual basis but also collectively, for your nation and for the world. I believe God is looking to the church to become effective in the critical situation that now confronts your nation.

You must look above the level of individual need, because, if your whole nation crumbles, your individual needs are going to look very small in the light of that catastrophe. We are at the point where such a catastrophe could easily happen. Divine intervention alone will prevent it, and the church of Jesus Christ is the only agency on earth to precipitate that divine intervention.

In previous chapters, we have learned about the place of fasting as a means of humbling ourselves so that we might avert God's judgment on our nation. I suppose that when fasting is practiced in accordance with the principles of God's Word, there is no greater weapon available to the people of God.

Let's now look at another tremendous weapon that God has put at our disposal as Christians so that we may gain the victory in the spiritual conflict in which we are engaged: the power of our witness.

TO THE UTTERMOST PART OF THE EARTH

In Acts 1:8, we read the last words Jesus spoke to His disciples while He was on earth:

> *But you shall receive power when the Holy Spirit has come upon you; and you shall be witnesses to Me in Jerusalem, and in all Judea and Samaria, and to the end ["uttermost part" KJV] of the earth.* (Acts 1:8)

This verse tells us that the primary purpose of our receiving the baptism of the Holy Spirit is to become witnesses. "*You shall be witnesses.*" Notice that Jesus did not say, "You shall witness." Some people are professional witnesses, but that is not what Jesus was talking about. He was talking about being a witness in everything we say and do. Our whole life is a witness.

Note also that we are to be witnesses *to Him*. We are not to be witnesses to an experience or to a denomination. We are to be witnesses to the Lord Jesus Christ. You will find that the Holy Spirit always begins to withdraw when people become witnesses to anything other than Jesus Christ. The Holy Spirit will move on from there because He has come to make us witnesses of one Person only, and that Person is the Lord Jesus Christ. The purpose of this witness of Jesus is to be extended to the uttermost part of the earth.

The outpouring of the Holy Spirit at Pentecost was like a great stone thrown into the middle of a pond. It produced a tremendous splash, but the splash was not the end. Out of that splash, ripples began to go outward in all directions, one wave after another. The purpose of God is that those ripples should go out from that great central splash until they have touched every margin of the pond—until they have reached the uttermost part of the earth.

THE OPPORTUNITIES GOD GIVES

I can never teach on Acts 1:8 without giving my personal testimony, which just happens to fit in so well with this topic. When I finally got out of the British Army after five and a half years (one year unconverted, then four and a half years converted), it was expected that I would go home. But that did not happen—I did not go back to Britain at that time.

The day I ceased to be a British soldier, I became a missionary—and not in the accepted, traditional way. I never went before a mission board or interviewed with anybody except the Lord. Essentially, the Lord told me that He had called me, and I proceeded with that call. The Bible says, *"He who calls you is faithful, who also will do it"* (1 Thessalonians 5:24). The Lord also told me very clearly that the door was open to full-time ministry at that time, and if I wished, I could step through it. If I waited, it would close.

There are two situations that never wait for man's convenience: God's opportunities and God's judgment. They never come when we feel ready for them. We must decide whether we will fit in with God or let Him move past us. God showed me this principle so clearly at that time.

TWO SITUATIONS NEVER WAIT FOR MAN'S CONVENIENCE: GOD'S OPPORTUNITIES AND GOD'S JUDGMENT.

My grandfather was at home, dying of cancer. My family had not seen me for four and a half years. I was the only grandson, the only male descendant of the entire family, so everybody thought it was logical that I would return home. The British Army was obligated and waiting to transport me home. Yet it was then that God said, *I have opened the door for ministry. You can go in now if you want to. But if you wait, the door will close.* That was a critical moment in my life—and I am so glad I stepped through the door that God opened.

So, I became a missionary. I started my preaching career in the city of Jerusalem in 1946. I praise the Lord that in the years that followed, I was able to go to the uttermost part of the earth as well. By the way, do you know where that "uttermost part" is? Remember, that point is to be measured from Jerusalem. If you look at a globe and measure the farthest distance on the earth's surface from Jerusalem to a place that is inhabited, that place is the east coast of New Zealand. There is no question about that.

During Christmas 1967, I made it to New Zealand, and I have been back there many times since then. My chief desire and objective was to be a witness to the uttermost part of the earth, until every tribe, nation, kingdom, and tongue had heard about the Lord Jesus Christ.

I am concerned that the church in general has been remarkably slack about reaching that objective. Out of hundreds of millions of people on the continent of Africa, many millions have never heard the name of Jesus. And if you go to the subcontinent of India, the proportion is similar.

"THE OLD, OLD STORY"

Years ago, I saw a picture in a magazine of an old Asian woman who was gray-haired, wrinkled, and stooped over. She said about the gospel, "The old, old story?! I'm old—and I have never even heard it once!" Are you familiar with the hymn "Tell Me the Old, Old Story"? There are lots of people like the old Asian woman who have never heard it once. For them, it is not an old story. For some people, it is startlingly new.

Once, when a friend of mine was on a flight to Russia, he began to testify to the stewardesses. Reading John 3:16 to them, he said, "God loves you." They said, "God loves us? Impossible. We have never heard this in our whole lives." He led those two stewardesses to the Lord in the airplane, right in front of the rest of the passengers. In all their lives, they had never heard that God loved them—it was totally new to them.

What are we here for? To be witnesses to Jesus Christ—to tell people, to let them know, to let them see.

We may do this in many different ways. I know some good people who can follow an evangelism method with great success. They get into an airplane, sit next to somebody, and—lo and behold—in ten minutes, they have shared the entire gospel with that person! Believe me, if I try to do that, it is a total failure. I just have to allow the Lord to let me be myself.

The way I witness to people could possibly be quite different from the way you would witness. But the people we are witnessing to know when it is real, so we have to be ourselves. I have discovered that if I am just natural in the Lord, I am a witness. One way or another, God will speak through me to people—provided I am prepared to let Him. So again, the primary purpose of our being here is to be witnesses of Jesus Christ.

AN UNFORGETTABLE SCENE

I mentioned that Jesus' words in Acts 1:8 were the last words that fell from His lips as He was about to leave earth and ascend into heaven. Have you ever actually thought about what that moment was like? You yourself know that when you say good-bye to somebody who is very dear to you, there is that moment of farewell that you treasure. It is imprinted on your memory like an inward photograph.

I remember when my wife and I said good-bye to one of our daughters and sons-in-law who were going with their little son to East Africa as missionaries. As we stood there and watched the train steam out of the station, it was a vivid scene. Every detail became imprinted on our minds.

I am sure that it was a vivid scene for Jesus' disciples when the Lord was taken from them. They knew that they would never see Him in that way again. Consequently, the last words that He spoke must have been particularly significant and sacred to them. Consider those final words: *"...the uttermost part of the earth"* (Acts 1:8 KJV). I am sure the disciples went home with those words echoing in their minds.

YOU ARE GOD'S PLAN, AND HE HAS NO ALTERNATIVE.

What captivated the heart of the Lord? The uttermost part of the earth. In effect, He was saying, "I've died. I've paid the penalty. The work is finished. But no one will benefit from it unless they hear about it. I might just as well never have died if men and women don't hear about My death on their behalf." Don't you think that is true? It is perfectly true.

Somebody once painted a word picture depicting the scene when the Lord got back to heaven. The angels were worshipping and welcoming Him, telling Him how wonderful all He had done was. Then one of the angels said to Him, "Lord, You have accomplished all this, You have paid the price, and You have made salvation possible. What is Your plan to get this message to the people who need it?" The Lord replied, "Well, I have some disciples down there." The angel inquired, "But You know how unreliable they have been. They have misunderstood You, they have failed You, they have denied You. Suppose they don't go and tell the people? What alternative plan do You have?" In response, the Lord said, "I have no alternative plan."

That is the reality today. *You* are God's plan, and He has no alternative. If you fail, the whole plan fails. We are His witnesses. The Bible says that. We can be distressed about the appalling events that are reported in the newspapers and the awful content that is shown on the movie screens. But those matters are not witnesses to Him. We are the ones whom He is relying on to make Him known to the world. Will we step up to that responsibility?

CHAPTER 19

THE POWER OF TESTIMONY AND PRAISE

We will now examine the further application of our testimony as a way to win a dying world to Jesus. The word of our testimony is a powerful spiritual weapon for the cause of Christ.

THE RULER OF THIS WORLD WAS CAST OUT

Let us begin by looking at the words Jesus said in preparation for going to the cross:

Now is the judgment of this world; now the ruler ["prince" KJV] of this world will be cast out. (John 12:31)

That is good news, isn't it? Through what Jesus did on the cross, the ruler, or prince, of this world—the devil—was cast out. At the cross, his path was stopped. He could not get beyond it. Let's tell the world our good news: The devil cannot get beyond the cross! He can't get over it. He can't get under it. He can't get around it. He can't get through it. His territory ends at the cross. He has been cast out by Jesus' death and resurrection.

Do you know what Jesus meant by the words *"Now is the judgment of this world"*? The people who demanded Jesus' death thought they were judging Him, but they were judging themselves. The judgment that came upon Jesus was the judgment that was due to them (and all of us). He was judged in their place. He was their Substitute. *"Now is the judgment of this world"*—and because the judgment of this world fell upon Jesus, the ruler of this world has been cast out. His authority is finished. He has no more claim over the "new man" in Christ Jesus.

As we have seen, Jesus was *"the last Adam"* (1 Corinthians 15:45). Then, when His work on the cross was finished, He became *"the second Man"* (verse 47)—the Head of a new race. He emerged through the resurrection on the right side of the cross, where there are no more shadows, where there is only the light of God's countenance. *"Now is the judgment of this world; now the ruler of this world will be cast out"* (John 12:31). I love that statement—it is a tremendously significant proclamation for us to absorb.

David prayed,

> *Draw out the spear, and stop those who pursue me* ["*stop the way against them that persecute me*" KJV]. *Say to my soul, "I am your salvation."*
> (Psalm 35:3)

The Lord answered that prayer at the cross. There, He said, "I am your salvation," and He stopped the way against the enemy of our soul. If you are living on the right side of the cross, you are out of Satan's territory.

BECAUSE OF THE CROSS

In that regard, let's also look at the first chapter of Colossians:

> [God] *hath delivered us from the power of darkness, and hath translated us into the kingdom of his dear Son.* (Colossians 1:13 KJV)

Translation is total. Two men in the Old Testament were "translated" to heaven without dying: Enoch and Elijah. (See Genesis 5:24; Hebrews 11:5; 2 Kings 2:1, 11–12.) Neither of them left his body behind. Their translation was entire, and so is ours.

God has translated us—spirit, soul, and body—out of the territory of darkness and into the kingdom of His dear Son, where the rules and the laws are the rules and laws of love. *"The law of the Spirit of life in Christ Jesus has made me free from the law of sin and death"* (Romans 8:2). This is not going to happen in the next age; it has happened now. Because of the cross, I have been translated out of the territory where I was under the laws of Satan, and I am now under the laws of the kingdom of God.

In dealing with people who need deliverance from evil spirits, I have discovered that the great weapon is the cross. Demons tremble when you know how to tell them about the cross. They tremble at the name of Jesus, the blood of Jesus, and the testimony of what Jesus did on the cross.

You do not need to be afraid of the devil. This may sound like a startling statement, but the Word of God says, *"Therefore submit to God. Resist the devil and he will flee from you"* (James 4:7).

LIFT UP THE LORD JESUS

After Jesus declared, *"Now the ruler of this world will be cast out"* (John 12:31), He said,

> *And I, if I am lifted up from the earth, will draw all peoples to Myself.* (John 12:32)

Whose business is it to lift up the Lord? Ours. I am convinced that if every Christian did his or her best to lift up the Lord, all people would be drawn to Him. That is not an exaggeration. I believe it to be the exact truth. I am not saying that *every person* would come to Him; some might still resist. Yet every individual, in all parts of the world, would feel the tug of the Holy Spirit to Jesus if you and I were doing our job.

What is that job? Lifting up the Lord Jesus Christ. That is what we are here for—not to promote a church or a denomination, not to give undue credit to the devil by what we say, but rather to lift up the Lord.

Unfortunately—and I say this without being critical—I think the majority of God's people spend more time advertising what the devil has done than they do advertising what the Lord has done. The average prayer meeting can become a long list of advertisements for the devil: "I've had this ailment, and my whole family has been ill." "My doctor says I have an incurable disease"—and so forth. Any semblance of lifting up the Lord is a thousand miles away from all that. The tragedy is that people fail to realize the destructive power of such negative testimony.

To counter that kind of activity, I will list for you some Scripture references that give us something positive to testify about. There is no problem getting Christians to talk—the key is getting them to talk about the right subjects.

THE RIGHT SUBJECTS

Our first reference is from the book of Psalms:

I will also meditate on all Your work, and talk of Your deeds.

(Psalm 77:12)

My dear friend, if you meditate on the right subject, you will talk about the right subject. The two go together.

Next, we will look at Joshua 1:8, where God told the Israelites:

This Book of the Law shall not depart from your mouth, but you shall meditate in it day and night, that you may observe to do according to all that is written in it. For then you will make your way prosperous, and then you will have good success.

The Bible does not tell you how to be a failure. It tells you how to succeed—and it is all there in this Scripture. Let's examine the first part of Joshua 1:8 more closely.

This Book of the Law shall not depart from your mouth, but you shall meditate in it day and night, that you may observe to do....

We are to take three directions: *think* the Word of God, *speak* the Word of God, and *act* the Word of God. Put these three actions into practice, and you are invulnerable. You cannot fail. God does not love Joshua any more than He loves you. If you do what Joshua was told to do, you will get the same results. It is what you meditate on and what you speak about that is decisive in your experience.

This is so true that even salvation depends on it. We see this clearly in Romans 10:9–10:

> *...that if you confess with your mouth the Lord Jesus and believe in your heart that God has raised Him from the dead, you will be saved. For with the heart one believes unto righteousness, and with the mouth confession is made unto salvation.*

You cannot be saved on the basis of a wrong confession. You must confess with your mouth the right truths. *To confess* means "to say the same as." This is vitally important. Confession for the believer is saying the same truths with your mouth that God has said in His Word.

This is reaffirmed to us in Philippians 4:8:

> *Finally, brethren, whatever things are true, whatever things are noble ["honest" KJV], whatever things are just, whatever things are pure, whatever things are lovely, whatever things are of good report, if there is any virtue and if there is anything praiseworthy; meditate on these things.*

Eight *"things"* to think about are given in this verse, and you will not find anything negative or discouraging in the list. They are all good. Somebody pointed out to me that certain birds feed on living flesh, and other birds feed on carrion. What this person expressed was very simple: Each type of bird finds what it is looking for. The bird that is looking for living flesh finds living flesh. The bird that is seeking rotten flesh finds rotten flesh.

Your mind is just the same—it will find what it is looking for. If you want to feed on ripe, juicy flesh, it is there. If you want to feed on carrion, it is there. You can feed on the good or the bad.

Paul said to *"meditate on these things."* Direct your mind. Your mind is not to be your master; it is your servant. You can cultivate the habit of thinking about the right things. It takes time, but remember that it is a commandment of the Word of God.

OUR DISTINGUISHING MARK

A verse that parallels this thought is also found in Philippians. It begins, *"For we are the circumcision…"* (Philippians 3:3). Circumcision is the mark of God's covenant people. In the Old Testament, the circumcision was in the flesh; but in the New Testament, it is in the heart. (See Romans 2:28–29.) Christians bear this distinguishing mark of New Testament circumcision if they are those *"who worship God in the Spirit, rejoice in Christ Jesus, and have no confidence in the flesh"* (Philippians 3:3). That is what it means to be circumcised with the circumcision of the new covenant. Everyone who does not have this mark does not belong.

"Worship God in the Spirit, rejoice in Christ Jesus…." We are to continually boast about the Lord Jesus. *Boast* is a very powerful word. Certainly, we have the option to talk about any subject. We can focus our conversation on social problems, education, or other topics. But at some point, we ought to be boasting about Jesus. The people of God, regardless of denomination—Catholic, Protestant, and others—ought to be talking about Jesus. That is the business of the church. We make our boast in the Lord. We ought to be very bold in glorifying the Lord Jesus Christ.

PRAISE IS A DECISION

I want you to notice that in Psalm 34, David made a decision as to what he was going to talk about. He said:

> I will bless the LORD at all times; His praise shall continually be in my mouth. My soul shall make its boast in the LORD; the humble shall hear of it and be glad. Oh, magnify the LORD with me, and let us exalt His name together. (Psalm 34:1–3)

David's decision left no room for complaining or murmuring or negative talk. You cannot have the praise of the Lord continually in your mouth and negative confessions in your mouth at the same time. It must be one or the other.

To magnify means "to make great," and *to exalt* means "to make high." This is the business of the church: to boast in the Lord Jesus, to make His name great and to exalt the Person of Christ. If we will do this, the whole atmosphere around us will change. In fact, this change in atmosphere will affect your community, your city, and your nation. This has been proven to be true.

Referring once again to the great Welsh Revival of 1904, God's people came together, testified about what He had done, and spent hours praising Him. Do you know what happened as a result? Every tavern was closed, every boxing match was canceled, and every football game ceased, because there were no spectators. We see clearly from biblical history that when God's people got busy doing what they should have been doing all along, God took care of their enemies. He took care of their social problems.

God can do it for us as well. When we win the victory in the Spirit, we have won the victory. Then we can just sit back and watch God deal with our enemies.

WHAT WE SHOULD SAY

In Psalm 71, we find other verses that tell us what we should be saying with our mouths. Bear in mind that I am giving you only short selections out of many possible passages.

Let my mouth be filled with Your praise and with Your glory all the day. (Psalm 71:8)

My lips shall greatly rejoice when I sing to You, and my soul, which You have redeemed. (Psalm 71:23)

My tongue also shall talk of Your righteousness all the day long. (Psalm 71:24)

"All the day" is a pretty long while. Next, let's read Psalm 105:1–3:

Oh, give thanks to the LORD! Call upon His name; make known His deeds among the peoples! Sing to Him, sing psalms to Him; talk of all His wondrous works! Glory in His holy name.

Notice the word *"Glory."* *To glory* means "to boast, to exalt, to be extremely confident." We are to *"talk of all [the Lord's] wondrous works."*

BY AN ACT OF OUR WILL, WE TAKE THE STEP TO THINK ABOUT AND SPEAK ABOUT THE GOODNESS AND FAITHFULNESS OF GOD.

Psalm 145:1–12, included below, is the last passage I will cite in this section. Once again, I would like you to notice the emphasis on decision. We need to be saying, very definitively, statements such as the following: "I will praise the Lord on Sunday morning," or "I will extol God on Tuesday evening"; "I will bless the Lord because I've made up my mind to do it"; "I will meditate on God's majesty and speak of His greatness, because I'm not going to be pushed around by every wind of circumstance. I have a mind and a will, and I can decide what I will think about and what I will talk about." By an act of our will—a decision—we take the step to think about and speak about the goodness and faithfulness of God. This is a powerful personal decision.

GLORIFY THE LORD

As a fitting close to this chapter, I would recommend that you proclaim aloud the words spoken to and about the Lord by the psalmist in Psalm 145. Please feel free to declare these words with vigor:

I will extol You, my God, O King; and I will bless Your name forever and ever. Every day I will bless You, and I will praise Your name forever and ever. Great is the LORD, and greatly to be praised; and His greatness is unsearchable. One generation shall praise Your works to another, and shall declare Your mighty acts. I will meditate on the glorious splendor of Your majesty, and on Your wondrous works. Men shall speak of the might of Your awesome acts, and I will declare Your greatness. They shall utter the memory of Your great goodness, and shall sing of Your righteousness. The LORD is gracious and full of compassion, slow to anger and great in mercy. The LORD is good to all, and His tender mercies are over all His works. All Your works shall praise You,

O LORD, and Your saints shall bless You. They shall speak of the glory of Your kingdom, and talk of Your power, to make known to the sons of men His mighty acts, and the glorious majesty of His kingdom.

(Psalm 145:1–12)

Verses 10–12 really sum up what I am trying to say. *"All Your works shall praise You, O LORD, and Your saints shall bless You...."* It is the saints, the people of God, who are going to do this.

When the Spirit of God fell on Jesus' disciples on the day of Pentecost, what were they all talking about? The answer is: *"the wonderful works of God"* (Acts 2:11). As a result, what happened? All Jerusalem came to find out what was going on. (See Acts 2:5–11.) If we make the same kinds of declarations, people will come. When we lift up the Lord, He will immediately begin to draw men to Himself.

Let's make it our aim and our resolution in all that we do and say to uplift and glorify the Lord Jesus Christ. Many times we will fail—especially at first. But we can simply ask the Lord to forgive us and then renew our commitment that we are going to be living advertisements for Jesus Christ.

The church has done enough advertising for the devil and his works. We have spoken far too often about what the enemy can do and what he has done. Instead, let's turn that process around to advertise the Lord. After all, He is worth advertising. His "products" are reliable. You can trust in them. And every one of them carries a written warranty. We can certainly praise the Lord for that!

As a matter of fact, why don't we do just that? To close this chapter, let's praise the Lord again by declaring the last three verses of the psalm we just read:

All Your works shall praise You, O LORD, and Your saints shall bless You. They shall speak of the glory of Your kingdom, and talk of Your power, to make known to the sons of men His mighty acts, and the glorious majesty of His kingdom. (Psalm 145:10–12)

CHAPTER 20

THE WORD OF OUR TESTIMONY

Before we have a further examination of our testimony for Christ, it will be helpful for us to briefly review what we have established so far about living as salt and light. We have learned that we are Christ's ambassadors, sent by Him into the world, just as He was sent by the Father to accomplish the Father's will and to demonstrate His power. We are God's personal representatives, restored to His likeness and invested with His authority. This is the position, the privilege, and the responsibility of the church.

FULFILLING OUR POSITION IN CHRIST

I am convinced that in almost every part of the body of Jesus Christ, there are people who are longing to fulfill their spiritual position. They just do not know how to do it. I have made it my sincere endeavor to educate Christians so that we can effectively engage in the spiritual conflict that is all around us—to win the battles for the Lord and to bring to pass the will of God in the earth.

In the introduction to this book, I mentioned a speaker I had heard who talked for almost an hour, telling how terrible the situation was in his country. Believe me, by the time he had finished, you knew it was bad! At the end, after all this bad news, he told the audience, almost in passing, that what we needed was a "Holy Spirit revival." However, I do not recall his giving one sentence of specific instruction as to how we could see that happen. I believe that the majority of the people who heard that message went away discouraged, depressed, and worried. "The situation is bad. We ought to do something. But what can we do?" Nobody knew.

In moments of crisis when everybody loses their heads, someone usually says, "Do something—somebody!" But you don't really get any results that way. I believe that the Bible makes it perfectly clear what we can do, and I think that many sincere Christians want to do it. That is my conviction.

To this end, the purpose of this book has been to present to you the basic truths about the spiritual weapons God has given to His people to change the course of events from bad to good—to dethrone satanic power and to enthrone, uplift, and exalt the Lord Jesus Christ.

BUILDING OUR ARSENAL

As we continue to review what we have already learned, let us focus on the building of our "arsenal" of spiritual weaponry. We examined what I labeled the "powerhouse of prayer," where two or three believers are gathered in harmonious agreement into the name of Jesus to wage spiritual warfare. We learned that this place of spiritual power must be fenced in by right relationships, protected from the damage of offenses between believing Christians.

OUR GOAL IS THAT THE WHOLE WORLD WILL FEEL THE DRAWING, ATTRACTING POWER OF THE LORD JESUS CHRIST.

We then took a serious look at fasting as a very powerful weapon. Our study was illustrated by personal, biblical, and historical examples in which fasting changed the course of history, prevented tragedy, deterred destruction, and, in some cases, even averted God's judgment.

Finally, in the chapters immediately preceding this one, we explored two additional weapons available to us as believers. The first is our witness, in fulfillment of Jesus' final instructions to the disciples before He ascended into heaven: *"And you shall be witnesses to Me...to the end* ["*uttermost part*" KJV] *of the earth*" (Acts 1:8). The second is found in the distinguishing covenantal mark we carry as New Testament Christians, which includes worshipping God in the Spirit and rejoicing in Christ Jesus. (See Philippians 3:3.) With the weapon of praise, we unleash the power of proclamation. We make a continual boast with our mouths about the Lord Jesus.

By our witness and our praise, we uplift and exalt the Lord Jesus, who said, "*And I, if I am lifted up from the earth, will draw all peoples to Myself*" (John 12:32). This is the primary purpose of our existence. Everything else is secondary. We may be here to raise a family, earn a living, fulfill a vocation, and experience other normal aspects of life. But those are all secondary purposes. The primary purpose for the Christian is to be a witness of the Lord Jesus Christ and to uplift Him in such a way that He will draw, by the Spirit, all people to Himself. Our goal is that the whole world will feel the drawing, attracting power of the Lord Jesus Christ.

DAYS OF CONFLICT

Let us now look at Revelation 12:7–11, a very significant passage that will be helpful for us. In this section of Scripture, there is a picture of the end-time conflict into which we have even now entered. I want to declare an important truth here: These last days are days of conflict. We will need our weapons of warfare.

I am reminded of this reality every time I read Psalm 55. Let's take just a moment to look at this psalm. David found himself involved in a conflict, and he said:

Indeed, I would wander far off, and remain in the wilderness. I would hasten my escape from the windy storm and tempest. (Psalm 55:7–8)

I believe many people could be feeling like David did, thinking to themselves, *I'd like to get out of this situation, but there isn't any way out. I must just embrace it and move forward by addressing it.* When David had come to this same conclusion, he turned on his enemies and prayed the words in Psalm 55:9: "*Destroy, O Lord, and divide their tongues....*"

In a previous chapter, I shared how I discovered this to be the most effective prayer concerning the forces that oppose God in the world today. I pray it every day. "Lord," I say, "You know the people who oppose You and resist You. You know the ones who reject You, Your Christ, Your Word, and Your Spirit—all those who oppose Your people and Your purposes in the earth. Now that I have identified them, this is my prayer: 'Destroy, O Lord, and divide their tongues.' Turn their tongues against one another."

I have found God faithful to answer this prayer. Nothing else is needed. Those enemies will overthrow themselves when we pray in that way. It is such a short, simple, effective prayer, and it undercuts their whole foundation.

It is clear that prior to praying this way in Psalm 55, David had a moment of fear. He cried out:

> *Give ear to my prayer, O God, and do not hide Yourself from my supplication. Attend to me, and hear me; I am restless in my complaint, and moan noisily, because of the voice of the enemy, because of the oppression of the wicked; for they bring down trouble upon me, and in wrath they hate me....Fearfulness and trembling have come upon me, and horror has overwhelmed me. So I said, "Oh, that I had wings like a dove! I would fly away and be at rest. Indeed, I would wander far off, and remain in the wilderness. I would hasten my escape from the windy storm and tempest."* (Psalm 55:1–3, 5–8)

David plainly wanted to get out of the circumstance he was facing. In the next verse, he said, *"For I have seen violence and strife in the city"* (Psalm 55:9). The whole scene confronting David was occupied by men of violence and strife. In that setting, David found the answer. It was not to run away but to turn and attack. So, he prayed, *"Destroy, O Lord, and divide their tongues."* Again, if God's people would pray like this, they would win the victory.

Actually, this one prayer alone has the potential to overthrow the forces of antichrist and atheism in the world today. I have prayed it, and I have seen it happen. We must all continue praying like this until the job is done. We do not need to run away. The Bible says to have courage, turn, and fight.

VICTORIOUS SAINTS

Now, as an introduction to the next chapter, let's turn our attention to our main Scripture, Revelation 12:7–11. The end-time conflict described here is not just a global conflict—it is a universal conflict. The scenario begins in verse 7:

> *And war broke out in heaven: Michael and his angels fought with the dragon; and the dragon and his angels fought, but they did not prevail, nor was a place found for them in heaven any longer. So the great dragon was cast out, that serpent of old, called the Devil and Satan, who deceives the whole world; he was cast to the earth, and his angels were cast out with him. Then I heard a loud voice saying in heaven, "Now salvation, and strength, and the kingdom of our God, and the power of His Christ have come, for the accuser of our brethren, who accused them before our God day and night, has been cast down. And they overcame him by the blood of the Lamb and by the word of their testimony, and they did not love their lives to the death."*
>
> (Revelation 12:7–11)

Notice the scope of this conflict: It involves heaven and earth, Michael and his angels, the devil and his angels, and the saints on earth. All are involved together in this one closing conflict. In the course of this massive struggle, the devil is dethroned from his realm of authority in the heavenlies and cast down to the earth. Without going into all the details of this situation, let us read the summary statement concerning his dethronement and his casting down, which is found in verse 11. It begins, *"And they overcame him...."*

If you examine the context of this phrase and study it for yourself, there is no doubt who *"they"* refers to—the saints on earth. *"They,"* the saints on earth, *"overcame him,"* the devil. Here is clear proof that we as Christians must be involved in direct conflict with Satan. It is person to person.

Please notice that although the archangels and the angels and the forces of heaven are involved, the final victory is won by the saints on earth. No one can say that we are unimportant.

OUR SECRET OF SPIRITUAL VICTORY

The victory that we win represents an amazing paradox. God has chosen the weak things and the base things to bring to naught the mighty. (See 1 Corinthians 1:27–28 KJV.) The angels are too mighty for the Lord to use as the ones who accomplish the final victory. This privilege has necessarily been given to us so that all the glory will go to the Lord.

CHRISTIANS MUST BE INVOLVED IN DIRECT CONFLICT WITH SATAN. IT IS PERSON TO PERSON.

In the following chapter, we will examine what is, in my opinion, one of the greatest secrets of spiritual victory anywhere in the Bible: How *they* overcame *him*. How did they overcome him? *"By the blood of the Lamb and by the word of their testimony"* (Revelation 12:11). Clearly, they were committed: *"They did not love their lives to the death"* (verse 11). As I mentioned earlier, they were like Esther. It did not matter whether they lived or died—that was not important.

This teaching is not for uncommitted Christians. It is for those who are determined to do the job, no matter what it costs. The exclamation in Esther 4:16—*"If I perish, I perish!"*—is the cry of the victorious Christian.

CHAPTER 21

OVERCOMING BY THE BLOOD

I now want to explain to you as clearly as possible what it means to overcome by the blood of the Lamb and by the word of your testimony. As I said at the end of chapter 20, I believe this is one of the greatest secrets of spiritual victory anywhere in the Bible. I have carefully considered the practical application of Revelation 12:11, and I have discovered it to be the most amazingly effective weapon you can imagine. I will paraphrase it in this way:

> You overcome Satan by the blood of the Lamb and by the word of your testimony when you testify personally as to what the Word of God says the blood of Jesus does for you.

We will examine this pivotal statement in detail.

Notice that you testify personally to the devil. This does not refer to a testimony meeting in which you stand up in front of the brothers and sisters in your church and say, "I'd like to give a praise report…." Those meetings can be wonderful, but that is not what I am talking about. Instead, you are testifying to the devil. You are testifying to what the Word of God says the blood of Jesus does for you. You are applying the blood to your situation.

THE PASSOVER LAMB

In the Old Testament, the Passover lamb was the greatest single type of Christ—the Lamb who was slain, who shed His blood. This connection is cited in many places in the New Testament. Paul said, "*Christ, our Passover, was sacrificed for us*" (1 Corinthians 5:7). John the Baptist said, "*Behold! The Lamb of God…*" (John 1:29), referring to Jesus as the Passover Lamb. But the Lamb of God does not take away the sin of just one household in Israel. This Lamb "*takes away the sin of the world*" (John 1:29).

Exodus 12 records the first Passover. You will find that each Hebrew household had to slay its own lamb, and the lamb's blood was caught in a basin. However, God said to Israel, in essence, "The blood will protect you only when it is struck upon the front of your house—upon the lintel and the two side doorposts." Then He said, "*When I see the blood, I will pass over you*" (Exodus 12:13).

Very simply and plainly, I want to bring this thought to you: The blood in the basin protected nobody. No Israelite was saved from wrath and judgment while the blood remained in the basin. Every Israelite family, by an act of their own volition and faith, had to transfer the blood from the basin to the place God had appointed, where it was publicly displayed for all to see—good and bad.

There was one God-appointed means by which they were to make this transfer—they were not to use any other. The means was a little herb called *hyssop*, which grows abundantly in the Middle East. They had to take a bunch of hyssop, dip it in the blood in the basin, and strike it upon the lintel and upon the two doorposts.

Please note that they did *not* put it on the threshold. We are not to walk over the blood. Also note that they were to strike it—it was to be a firm, decisive act.

Faith is not an experiment. It is not "I will see if this works." A lot of people *try* divine healing, for instance. But a very great preacher of divine healing, Lilian Yeomans, who was a medical doctor, said, "You don't try divine healing. Divine healing tries you." And that is the truth.

So, this application of the blood was not an experiment. It was a decisive act of obedience. The Israelites took the blood and struck it upon the lintel and the doorposts. When they did that and remained behind the blood all through the hours of darkness, they were safe.

A PATTERN FOR US

The procedure the Israelites followed is given to us by the Lord as a pattern—its results are true for us as well. Christ, our Passover, has been slain for us. (See 1 Corinthians 5:7.) Figuratively, the blood is in the basin. But the blood in the basin is of no avail. It does not protect one person. You must apply it individually, personally, with your own act of faith, before it becomes effective. You have to transfer the blood from the basin to the place where it is publicly displayed over your life. Then it is a protection for you.

THE BLOOD OF THE LAMB AND THE WORD OF YOUR TESTIMONY ARE APPLIED WHEN YOU MAKE THE RIGHT STATEMENT ABOUT THE BLOOD.

Under the old covenant, God appointed a bunch of hyssop as the means for getting the blood from the basin to the doorposts. Under the new covenant, we don't use hyssop—but we do use something that is available to every person, just as hyssop was readily available to the Israelites. Do you know what it is? The tongue. It is the words of our mouth that will transfer the blood from the basin.

The blood of the Lamb and the word of your testimony are applied when you make the right statement about the blood. That declaration takes the blood from the basin and puts it over your home and over your life. That is what is meant by *"They overcame him by the blood of the Lamb and by the word of their testimony"* (Revelation 12:11).

WHAT THE WORD TEACHES

In order to apply the blood in this way, you have to know what the Word teaches about the blood. If you are ignorant of what the Word teaches, it is impossible to do it. I am going to lead you through some Scriptures and statements from the Word of God about the blood of Jesus and explain how to apply them personally. Then, at the close of this chapter, I will summarize them as a proclamation you can use anytime you feel the need to testify to the blood of Jesus, and thereby overcome the devil.

We will begin with Ephesians 1:7:

In Him we have redemption through His blood, the forgiveness of sins, according to the riches of His grace.

Notice that your redemption is positional. It is only *in Christ*— "*in Him we have redemption.*" If you are not in Christ, you don't have redemption. To be redeemed means "to be bought back." We are bought back by Christ's blood. It is like a ransom that has been paid. When a person is kidnapped, the family may pay hundreds of thousands of dollars to "buy back" the loved one. For the sinner who has been captured by Satan, Jesus paid the ransom. The price was His blood. Through the blood, we are bought back out of the hand of the devil.

There are two tremendous statements about the blood in the above verse: "*through His* [Jesus'] *blood,*" and "*we have redemption.*" Now I will show you how to make this personal—how to take the "bunch of hyssop" and start striking those statements over your life. Say, "Through the blood of Jesus, I am redeemed." You may want to apply this truth by saying it out loud (if you are able to): "Through the blood of Jesus, I am redeemed."

A verse that perfectly complements this declaration from Ephesians 1:7 is Psalm 107:2, which begins, "*Let the redeemed of the* LORD *say so....*" You see, you are not redeemed until you *say so.* "Believing in the heart" is wonderful, but "confessing with the mouth" is salvation. (See Romans 10:9–10.) You can believe it—yet until you say so, you do not have it.

The second part of Psalm 107:2 says, "*...whom He has redeemed from the hand of the enemy.*" I have no doubts as to where I was—I was in the hand of the enemy. But through the blood of Jesus, I have been redeemed out of the enemy's hand. It is my delight to say so: "Through the blood of Jesus, I am redeemed out of the hand of the devil. I am not in his hand any longer." That is my first testimony.

"MY SINS ARE FORGIVEN"

Returning to Ephesians 1:7, we have seen that the first tremendous statement Scripture makes is that we are redeemed. Second, it says that we also have forgiveness of sins through the blood of Jesus. Without the shedding of blood, there is no remission of sin. (See Hebrews 9:22.) The second testimony we speak is this: "Through the blood of Jesus, all my sins are forgiven." I like to add that one little word of three letters— *all*—because it makes all the difference. "Through the blood of Jesus, *all* my sins are forgiven."

Another Scripture we will use in testifying to what the blood of Jesus does for us is in 1 John:

> *But if we walk in the light as He is in the light, we have fellowship with one another, and the blood of Jesus Christ His Son* [continually, regularly, permanently] *cleanses us from all sin.*   (1 John 1:7)

In the original Greek, the word translated *"cleanses"* is in what is known as the continual present tense. That means that as long as we are continually walking in the light (a condition we must meet), the blood of Jesus Christ is cleansing us now and continually from all sin. That is part of our testimony against the accusations of the enemy: "The blood of Jesus Christ, God's Son, is cleansing me now from all sin."

Our next testimony is taken from Romans:

> *Much more then, having now been justified by His blood, we shall be saved from wrath through Him.*   (Romans 5:9)

We are justified by the blood of Jesus. *Justified* means "made just or righteous." We have been made righteous by Jesus' blood. Therefore, this is how we testify using Romans 5:9: "Through the blood of Jesus, the righteousness of Christ is imputed to me by faith."

An additional dimension of our righteousness is found in 2 Corinthians. This verse tells us that Jesus became sin for us so that we might receive His righteousness:

> For He [God] made Him [Jesus] who knew no sin to be sin for us, that we might become the righteousness of God in Him.
> (2 Corinthians 5:21)

Christ is the source of my righteousness every day. It is not my own righteousness. I am not righteous by doing the best that I can do. My righteousness is the spotless righteousness of Jesus Christ, which I receive through His blood.

JUSTIFIED, SANCTIFIED

Based on Romans 5:9 and 2 Corinthians 5:21, we can testify in the following way: "Through the blood of Jesus, I am justified, made righteous, 'just-as-if-I'd' never sinned." That is what justification really means. It is just as if I'd never sinned. Anything less than that is condemnation. The only righteousness by which we can boldly approach the throne of God is the righteousness that is just as if we'd never sinned.

"THROUGH THE BLOOD OF JESUS, I AM JUSTIFIED, MADE RIGHTEOUS, 'JUST-AS-IF-I'D' NEVER SINNED."

All my sins are blotted out. God says He will remember them no more. (See Jeremiah 31:34.) I am clothed with a spotless garment of salvation and a robe of righteousness. (See Isaiah 61:10; Ephesians 5:27.)

Hebrews 13 provides another dimension of the blood of Jesus to which we can personally testify. This verse tells us that we are sanctified by the blood of Jesus:

> Therefore Jesus also, that He might sanctify the people with His own blood, suffered outside the gate. (Hebrews 13:12)

Clearly, to be sanctified is to be made holy. The significance of these words has become obscured, but there is no question about the literal meaning. God showed me in my study of Scripture that just as you can have the assurance of salvation, you can have the assurance of holiness. We need to know that it is by faith. By faith, you can reckon yourself holy, if you meet God's conditions.

Here is how we use this concept to testify: "Through the blood of Jesus, I am sanctified, made holy, set apart to God." The Lord repeatedly told the Egyptian pharaoh concerning His people Israel, "I will put a redemptive difference between My people and your people." (See Exodus 8:22; 9:4.) That redemptive difference is what comes between the devil and me. What is it? The blood of Jesus. I don't belong in the devil's territory. Through the blood of Jesus, I have been translated out of the power of darkness and into the kingdom of the Son of God's love. (See Colossians 1:13 KJV.)

A BOLD CONFESSION

God expects us to be very bold—provided we are doing it for the right reason. It is not bragging about what you or your church or your denomination have accomplished. Rather, it is about what God says the blood of Jesus does for you. You can never be too outspoken about that because, by your boldness, you are giving all the glory and honor to the Lord Jesus Christ.

We can combine all of the Scriptures we have covered so far, which are so significant in their implications, into one powerful confession. Let me give you the following example. (At the end of the chapter, I will provide a summary series of confessions, along with their corresponding Scripture references, to use in combined form as a bold testimony.)

Through the blood of Jesus, I have redemption.

I am redeemed by the blood of Jesus out of the hand of the devil.

Through the blood of Jesus, all my sins are forgiven.

The blood of Jesus Christ is continually cleansing me from all sin.

Through the blood of Jesus, I am justified, made righteous, just-as-if-I'd never sinned.

Through the blood of Jesus, I am sanctified, made holy, set apart to God.

In my experience of praying with people for deliverance, I have found that if there is one form of testimony the devil really dislikes, it is this type of confession. It is remarkable how the devil reacts against it. When the Spirit of God is moving, and the right confession is made, the devil will get so stirred up that his agitation in the person who needs deliverance will be obvious to all.

Please understand that the confession we have compiled is not to be used as just a routine or as a formula. It has to be lived out in the Spirit.

I read a book by a former rabbi who had somehow become a spiritist medium but later came into a salvation experience in Christ and received the baptism of the Holy Spirit. In his book, he pointed out that the devil is not the least bit afraid of people talking about the blood of Jesus if they do not do so in the power of the Holy Spirit.

There is no safe formula that will get you by. It is only by the presence of the power and anointing of the Holy Spirit that our testimony becomes effective.

BY WATER AND BLOOD

In the next section, we will add to the list of powerful testimonies we can declare concerning what God's Word says the blood of Jesus does for us. However, let me first point out what John stated about how the Holy Spirit bears witness to Jesus: *"This is He who came by water and blood; Jesus Christ; not only by water, but by water and blood. And it is the Spirit who bears witness, because the Spirit is truth"* (1 John 5:6). Certainly, Jesus came by water as the Great Teacher. Even before He went to the cross, He said to His disciples:

You are already clean because of the word which I have spoken to you.
(John 15:3)

Yet it is very important for us to understand that Jesus did not come only as the Great Teacher (as a lot of cults would lead you to believe). He also came as the Great Redeemer, to lay down His life as a substitutionary sacrifice and to shed His redeeming blood. This is what the Holy Spirit testifies to. Jesus came by water—but not by water only. He came by water and by blood. It is the Holy Spirit who bears witness both to the water of the Word and to the blood of the sacrifice.

IT IS ONLY BY THE PRESENCE OF THE POWER AND ANOINTING OF THE HOLY SPIRIT THAT OUR TESTIMONY BECOMES EFFECTIVE.

When the Holy Spirit begins to bear witness to Jesus and what He accomplished, believe me, all hell trembles. Moreover, the results are truly fantastic. I have seen people delivered from twenty or thirty evil spirits, one after another, when they have made this testimony. At first, when some of the people tried to make this declaration about the blood of Jesus, the demonic spirit would not even let them say the words. It would choke them. But as we would begin to plow through with the testimony, one after another, these evil spirits would come out.

THE POWER OF PROCLAMATION

Here is another dynamic statement that can be added to our combined confession: "My body is a temple for the Holy Spirit, redeemed, cleansed, and sanctified by the blood of Jesus. The devil has no place in me; the devil has no power over me." (See 1 Corinthians 6:19; Revelation 5:9; John 14:30; Luke 10:19.)

Each of the above sentences is absolutely scriptural. Accordingly, when the Spirit of God moves you to begin saying them, you will start to see tremendous results.

You may want to keep saying these sentences over and over—not because merely repeating them will bring about a change but because, as you say them, you will grow in faith and belief.

These are powerful truths, and there is an advantage to learning them by heart. How do you do that? By repeating the statements with your mouth. As you say them out loud, they get down into your heart, where they become operative. That is why, in talking about salvation in Romans 10:9, Paul did not put "believing" first. He put "confessing" first. Paul's approach may be contrary to our thinking, but he said:

> *If you confess with your mouth the Lord Jesus and believe in your heart that God has raised Him from the dead, you will be saved.*
>
> (Romans 10:9)

Interestingly, in the next verse, Paul stated,

> *For with the heart one believes unto righteousness, and with the mouth confession is made unto salvation.* (Romans 10:10)

"IF I WANT TO BELIEVE
SOMETHING IN THE WORD
OF GOD, I START TO
SAY IT OUT LOUD."

If you are not quite sure whether you believe something, start saying it. When you say it, you will believe it. Smith Wigglesworth had a healing and evangelistic ministry during the first half of the twentieth century. In so many ways, he had a simple approach that was full of tremendous insight. When he would quote Romans 9, he would also quote Romans 10:17, which says, *"So then faith comes by hearing, and hearing by the word of God."* He concluded, "If I want to believe something in the Word of God, I start to say it out loud. As I listen to myself saying it, I begin to believe it." This practice is perfectly logical and scriptural. It is not silly by any means.

LINKING THE SCRIPTURES

I promised that at the end of this chapter, I would give you a summary series of confessions and their corresponding Scriptures for you to combine to use as a bold testimony. Here they are:

- Through the blood of Jesus, I am redeemed out of the hand of the devil. Through the blood of Jesus, all my sins are forgiven. (See Ephesians 1:7.)

- The blood of Jesus Christ, God's Son, is cleansing me now from all sin. (See 1 John 1:7.)

- Through the blood of Jesus, I am justified, made righteous, just-as-if-I'd never sinned. (See Romans 5:9.)

- Through the blood of Jesus, I am sanctified, made holy, set apart to God. (See Hebrews 13:12.)

- My body is a temple for the Holy Spirit, redeemed, cleansed, and sanctified by the blood of Jesus. The devil has no place in me and no power over me. (See 1 Corinthians 6:19; Revelation 5:9; John 14:30; Luke 10:19.)

This is a series of words of testimony (though not an exhaustive list) that we can proclaim. By them, we testify to the power of the blood of Jesus, and thereby overcome the devil himself.

Testimony is a potent weapon, part of an arsenal we can employ to win complete victory by totally spiritual means. To affirm that victory, let's conclude with a declaration of the triumph we obtain by the weapons that God has provided for us. If you are able to proclaim this passage out loud, please do:

For though we walk in the flesh, we do not war according to the flesh. For the weapons of our warfare are not carnal but mighty in God for pulling down strongholds. (2 Corinthians 10:3–4)

Let's proclaim it once more as we bring this chapter to a close:

For the weapons of our warfare are not carnal but mighty in God for pulling down strongholds.

CHAPTER 22

AGAINST ALL ODDS

After making such powerful proclamations in the previous chapter, are you ready to study a biblical event where similar proclamations brought total victory? We find the story in 2 Chronicles 20. It describes a situation in the Old Testament in which the king of Judah and his people gained a complete military victory without the use of a single "carnal," or material, weapon. It was a victory that came through the application of nothing but spiritual weapons.

Before we examine this story, let me point out that under the old covenant, it was normal and acceptable to God that His people should use material weapons of war, because that was part of the dispensation in which they lived. Of course, they also needed to be in right relationship with God and to follow His directions in order to obtain a victory. Yet there were times when God called them to employ purely spiritual weapons, such as praise and shouting, in the process of defeating their enemies.

Under the new covenant, according to Ephesians 6:12, we do not wrestle against flesh and blood. We are not fighting human beings but evil principalities and powers. Therefore the weapons of our warfare are not carnal, as we just proclaimed from 2 Corinthians 10:3–4. If, under the old covenant, God's people could win total military victory by employing spiritual weapons, how much more should this apply to us who are living in the New Testament age and dispensation in which it is entirely appropriate and scriptural?

A PATTERN OF SPIRITUAL WARFARE

Let's turn our attention now to the account in 2 Chronicles 20. I will begin by briefly giving the background for how this biblical event took place. The main character of the story is Jehoshaphat, a righteous king and the leader of God's people in the southern kingdom of Judah.

WHEN WE TURN AWAY FROM FEAR BY TURNING TO GOD, HE BRINGS SOLUTIONS TO THE DILEMMAS WE FACE.

Jehoshaphat was informed that a tremendous enemy army was advancing and invading the kingdom from the east. He realized immediately that his nation did not have the military resources or the numbers to resist and overcome this alien army.

Recognizing this reality, Jehoshaphat turned entirely to the spiritual realm. By utilizing a series of spiritual weapons, he and his people obtained total victory—to the extent that they never had to shoot an arrow, cast a spear, or wield a sword. All they had to do was take the spoils from the dead bodies of their enemies. Not one of their enemies escaped alive, so they got all the plunder of war. The only labor they had was three days spent in gathering the spoil, because there was so much of it. If that is not total victory, I don't know what it is.

This story is an almost perfect pattern of spiritual warfare—applicable to God's people today. There is not one sentence of this account that is out-of-date. If God's people will take the same kind of action, they will obtain the same results.

TURNING TO GOD

Jehoshaphat was a great king, but he was also a human being like us. This is the record of his reaction when he was told that an invading army was on the way: *"Jehoshaphat feared"* (2 Chronicles 20:3). Jehoshaphat was a man, but he was not a foolish man. He looked facts in the face, and he realized there was good cause for fear in the natural realm.

The same is true today. In certain respects, we might say that the forces of evil could be overwhelming to us. It is not inappropriate to fear. We must be objective and see situations as they are. Yet when we turn away from fear by turning to God, He brings solutions to the dilemmas we face. Incorporated in the victory we read about in this story is the use of some of the same spiritual weaponry that has been our focus throughout this book.

STEPS TO VICTORY

Beginning with Jehoshaphat's reaction to the crisis, let's explore the steps to victory that unfold in this passage.

1. FASTING

And Jehoshaphat feared, and set himself to seek the LORD, and proclaimed a fast throughout all Judah. (2 Chronicles 20:3)

Weapon number one in this story is fasting. This weapon has been employed by God's people all through the ages. In moments of crisis, His people have always known that fasting is the way they should respond.

2. GATHERING

So Judah gathered together to ask help from the LORD; and from all the cities of Judah they came to seek the LORD. (2 Chronicles 20:4)

The next great tactical move was to get God's people together. Such a coming together is what He also requires of us. He is no longer blessing people who are out merely to promote their own particular churches or add to their numbers of members. You just cannot get God to bless what He is not interested in blessing. But if you start to do what God wants you to do, you will be amazed at how He will bless.

If you are going to be put in prison for being a Christian, it is not going to be very important whether you are imprisoned for being a Methodist or a Baptist or a Roman Catholic. We can see how the Spirit is moving all over the world in so many diverse settings, because God is not too concerned with denominations. All He wants is a platform on which to gather His people together.

Interestingly, the gathering He inspires is initiated by laypeople, not by churches or ministers. We see so many lay organizations through which God is moving and upon which He is pouring out His Spirit.

Years ago, for one of my trips to New Zealand and Australia, it was mainly laypeople who organized the meetings and brought the many denominations together. God is not interested in the labels or the status of those who are meeting—but He is looking for a platform on which His people can meet. So, the second great step in Judah's victory under Jehoshaphat is that they gathered themselves together.

3. PRAYER/TESTIMONY

We find the third great step in 2 Chronicles 20, beginning with verse 5:

Then Jehoshaphat stood in the assembly of Judah and Jerusalem, in the house of the LORD, before the new court, and said: "O LORD God of our fathers...." (2 Chronicles 20:5–6)

Jehoshaphat prayed. We will not include his entire prayer here, which continues for seven verses—but it is a model prayer. Why? Because he prayed entirely on the basis of the written Word of God. Jehoshaphat reminded God of His Word and His promises. Then he said, in effect, "Now we are holding You to what You have promised."

As I have often taught in regard to the prayer of David in 1 Chronicles 17, the key is in what David said in verse 23: *"And now, O LORD,...do as You have said."* When you can hold the Lord to what He has said, you can be assured He is going to do it. However, if you pray in ignorance of the written Word of God, your prayer will be weak and uncertain. There is no way around it; you must know the Scriptures. For example, you cannot testify to what the Word says about the blood if you don't know what the Word says. You cannot pray on the basis of the Word if you do not know the Word.

Jehoshaphat knew the Word of God. He knew the revelation existent in his day, and he prayed on the basis of that revelation. He reminded God of historical events. He reminded God of His promises. Then he said, in essence, "Now, Lord, it's up to You."

4. THE MOVING OF THE SPIRIT

In the fourth phase, we encounter the miraculous, supernatural manifestation of the Holy Spirit. After they had fasted, after they had come together, and after they had prayed—then came the prophecy.

> *Then the Spirit of the LORD came upon Jahaziel the son of Zechariah, the son of Benaiah, the son of Jeiel, the son of Mattaniah, a Levite of the sons of Asaph, in the midst of the assembly. And he said, "Listen, all of you Judah and you inhabitants of Jerusalem, and you, King Jehoshaphat! Thus says the LORD to you...."* (2 Chronicles 20:14–15)

The Spirit of the Lord came upon Jahaziel. Therefore, it was not Jahaziel talking. It was God talking through him. What God said was a directive word of edification, exhortation, comfort, and direction. It was an exhortation—but it was also comforting. It was not condemnatory; it was encouraging. Frankly, I am not looking for people to prophesy words of condemnation over me. I have enough sources of discouragement without people prophesying discouragement over me.

The first words spoken to Jehoshaphat from the Lord were these: *"Do not be afraid nor dismayed because of this great multitude..."* (2 Chronicles 20:15).

How many times have we read in the Scriptures that God said to His people, "Be not afraid!"? I am told that this phrase appears three hundred and sixty-five times in the Bible. That is once for every day of the year.

And how many times have we ourselves heard God say to us, "Don't be afraid"? The first time I received a personal message of prophecy, I was lying on the floor of a military ambulance, moving up across the western desert of North Africa to the front line in preparation for the battle of El Alamein. At the time, I was somewhat apprehensive, wondering what would happen. Immediately, I felt this wonderful burning in my stomach, and I thought, *Now I'm going to speak with tongues.* Yet out came the message in the form of a prophecy. The Lord said, *Thou shalt not be afraid.* God's very first words to me were encouraging ones: *You will not be afraid.*

We see the same kind of prophetic message continuing in verse 15:

> *Do not be afraid nor dismayed because of this great multitude, for the battle is not yours, but God's.*   (2 Chronicles 20:15)

A GENUINE PROPHECY
WILL BE QUICKENING,
STIMULATING, AND
IN LINE WITH THE
PURPOSES OF GOD.

After that marvelously encouraging word, there came some specific direction as to how they were to go forth, where they would meet the enemy, and what the enemy was doing. We will not need to go into all those details. You can read them for yourself in 2 Chronicles 20:16–17.

Then comes the people's response to this revelation. It is clear from their response that the revelation they had received from the Lord was life-giving. It quickened them, and it changed the atmosphere. Genuine prophetic utterances don't leave you feeling as if a wet blanket has been thrown over you. Real prophetic words quicken you—and they make the air electric. That is a good test of whether a prophetic word is authentic. A genuine prophecy will be quickening, stimulating, and in line with the purposes of God.

> *And Jehoshaphat bowed his head with his face to the ground, and all Judah and the inhabitants of Jerusalem bowed ["fell" KJV] before the LORD, worshipping the LORD.*   (2 Chronicles 20:18)

It would be easy to miss the magnitude of what occurred here. You could read verse 18 half a dozen times without picturing what it means for several thousand people to simultaneously fall to the ground. (In many churches today, such a response would be considered out of order.)

Why do people fall under the power of God? This story gives us an example. It was not because some minister said, "Now, let's all get down on our knees." Instead, something moved into that assembly and upon the people in such a way that they just could not stand in the presence of it.

In other places in the Bible, we read about when the glory of the Lord came into the temple of Solomon. At these times, the priests could not stand to minister by reason of the force of the glory of the Lord. After all, the Scriptures testify that all flesh is grass, and that when the wind of the Spirit blows upon the grass, the grass withers and the flower fades away. (See Isaiah 40:6–8.) Our flesh simply withers in the presence of the Spirit of God.

5. PRAISE

What happened next? We have only one more weapon to cover, and it is entirely sufficient. It is praise:

> *Then the Levites of the children of the Kohathites and of the children of the Korahites stood up to praise the LORD God of Israel with voices loud and high.* (2 Chronicles 20:19)

I am grateful for the loud voices—are you? Some people tell me, "I praise the Lord in my house." That is certainly wonderful, but we should not keep it just at home. Let it come out. In the appropriate seasons, we all ought to praise the Lord together with a loud voice. I am not very skilled at singing, but my voice is pretty loud, and I am always prepared to use it for the Lord.

> *So they rose early in the morning and went out into the Wilderness of Tekoa; and as they went out, Jehoshaphat stood and said* [he gave them a word of encouragement], *"Hear me, O Judah and you inhabitants*

of Jerusalem: Believe in the LORD your God, and you shall be estab-
lished; believe His prophets, and you shall prosper." And when he had
consulted with the people, he appointed those who should sing to the
LORD, and who should praise the beauty of holiness, as they went out
before the army and were saying: "Praise the LORD; for His mercy
endures forever." (2 Chronicles 20:20–21)

By modern military standards, the singers might have been considered superfluous and in the way. But actually, that was the key to the
whole victory—praise. Please take special note of what is contained in
the next two verses:

Now when they began to sing and to praise, the LORD set ambushes
against the people of Ammon, Moab, and Mount Seir, who had come
against Judah; and they were defeated. For the people of Ammon and
Moab stood up against the inhabitants of Mount Seir to utterly kill and
destroy them. And when they had made an end of the inhabitants of
Seir, they helped to destroy one another. (2 Chronicles 20:22–23)

This result is an exact outworking of the prayer I mentioned earlier:
"Destroy, O Lord, and divide their tongues" (Psalm 55:9). They turned
against one another. How many situations are there in which we should
perhaps just stand back, pray, and then wait to see what will come out
of it?

As we examine the story of Jehoshaphat and the people of Judah,
the question that arises is this: When did victory become effective? The
answer: When they began to sing and to praise—that is when the Lord
dealt with their enemy.

TO THE UNSUNG HEROES

Here is the final result of their prayer and praise:

And when Judah came toward the watch tower in the wilderness, they
looked unto the multitude, and, behold, they were dead bodies fallen to
the earth, and none escaped. (2 Chronicles 20:24 KJV)

I believe it is significant that the enemy got as far as the watch tower in the wilderness. I would like to give you a spiritual thought about that. The "watch tower" is the place where some child of God has kept watch in prayer and in spiritual vigil. I believe that in every nation of the world today, there are a number of consecrated saints whose names we may never know. They have taken their stand on the watch tower like the prophet Habakkuk, and they have said, as he did, *"I will stand my watch and set myself on the rampart..."* (Habakkuk 2:1). That is the place where the enemy is going to be stopped. While these saints are holding out, the body of God's people are grouping themselves for the victory.

THE "WATCH TOWER" IS THE PLACE WHERE SOME CHILD OF GOD HAS KEPT WATCH IN PRAYER AND IN SPIRITUAL VIGIL.

I do not know how to pay sufficient tribute to those precious, consecrated saints of God who, in spite of all the falling away, the apostasy, and the carnality in the church, have held on to the Lord day and night in prayer. I do not doubt that they are found throughout every nation and in every land. When the victory is won, we will discover that the enemy was stopped at the watch tower.

Oh, dear friend and faithful saint of God, if you are on a watch tower, just stay there a little while longer. Help is on the way. Don't give up. Only in the resurrection will you get your medal—but it will be a wonderful one.

People on earth may not perceive or appreciate the sacrifice you are now making. Many, many people who have benefitted from your prayers will never know anything about you until eternity. Nevertheless, hold out and continue in your vigilance.

Some decades ago, in the Hebrides, a chain of islands off the west coast of Scotland, there was a tremendous revival. Our daughter Elizabeth visited the places where this revival took place. There was an especially powerful move of God in an area called Lewis. In that vicinity, every tavern and every dance hall closed, because all the people who used to go to the taverns and the dance halls were in the prayer meetings. (What is the good of keeping a tavern open if everybody is in the prayer meeting?)

This revival began in 1949 and continued for several years. It is an established historical fact. I have heard Duncan Campbell, who was the minister God used in this revival, describe it firsthand.

But do you know what provoked the revival? The prayers of two old ladies, both over eighty. They held on to God day and night, year after year. They said, "God, You're a covenant-keeping God. We hold You to Your covenant." They didn't wait for everybody to be convinced. So you see, two convinced people can change the situation: "Where two or three are gathered..." (Matthew 18:20). God never really does anything astounding by the majority—He always uses the minority.

CHANGING OUR WORLD

Victory is intended for the people of God. It is our destiny. It never was otherwise. Not only that, but it is also in our power through the spiritual methods and weapons God has given us—prayer, fasting, testimony, and praise. There are other weapons available to us as well. But, believe me, when we are using even those that have been outlined in this book, they will prove sufficient to win the victory.

I want to challenge and encourage you to go and do something about the victory God intends for you and your nation. Don't wait for the whole church to be convinced. If you are convinced, find somebody else who is convinced, and start together—just the two of you. You plus one or two others in agreement can change the world.

If it is your desire to be a vital part of changing your nation and the world around you, I would invite you to express that desire with the following prayer:

Lord, I am convinced by everything I have examined in this book that You have given me the weapons, in concert and harmony with my brothers and sisters in Christ, to effect change in my nation and my world.

I volunteer myself now to be used by You—to join with others of like mind and to put these spiritual weapons to good use. By Your grace, and with Your help, I will fight against the forces of darkness and be victorious, using all that You have placed in my hands.

Thank You in advance, Lord, for the marvelous victory You will bring. I give all thanks and praise to You. I pray all these things in the name of our Lord and Savior, Jesus Christ, whose victory, already won on Calvary, we are enforcing in these significant days. Amen.

ABOUT THE AUTHOR

Derek Prince (1915–2003) was born in India of British parents. He was educated as a scholar of Greek and Latin at Eton College and King's College, Cambridge in England. Upon graduation he held a fellowship (equivalent to a professorship) in Ancient and Modern Philosophy at King's College. Prince also studied Hebrew, Aramaic, and modern languages at Cambridge and the Hebrew University in Jerusalem. As a student, he was a philosopher and self-proclaimed agnostic.

While in the British Medical Corps during World War II, Prince began to study the Bible as a philosophical work. Converted through a powerful encounter with Jesus Christ, he was baptized in the Holy Spirit a few days later. Out of this encounter, he formed two conclusions: first, that Jesus Christ is alive; second, that the Bible is a true, relevant, up-to-date book. These conclusions altered the whole course of his life, which he then devoted to studying and teaching the Bible as the Word of God.

Discharged from the army in Jerusalem in 1945, he married Lydia Christensen, founder of a children's home there. Upon their marriage, he immediately became father to Lydia's eight adopted daughters—six Jewish, one Palestinian Arab, and one English. Together, the family saw the rebirth of the state of Israel in 1948. In the late 1950s, they adopted another daughter while Prince was serving as principal of a teacher training college in Kenya.

In 1963, the Princes immigrated to the United States and pastored a church in Seattle. In 1973, Prince became one of the founders of Intercessors for America. His book *Shaping History through Prayer and Fasting* has awakened Christians around the world to their responsibility to pray for their governments. Many consider underground translations of the book as instrumental in the fall of communist regimes in the USSR, East Germany, and Czechoslovakia.

Lydia Prince died in 1975, and Prince married Ruth Baker (a single mother to three adopted children) in 1978. He met his second wife, like his first wife, while she was serving the Lord in Jerusalem. Ruth died in December 1998 in Jerusalem, where they had lived since 1981.

Until a few years before his own death in 2003 at the age of eighty-eight, Prince persisted in the ministry God had called him to as he traveled the world, imparting God's revealed truth, praying for the sick and afflicted, and sharing his prophetic insights into world events in the light of Scripture. Internationally recognized as a Bible scholar and spiritual patriarch, Derek Prince established a teaching ministry that spanned six continents and more than sixty years. He is the author of more than fifty books, six hundred audio teachings, and one hundred video teachings, many of which have been translated and published in more than one hundred languages. He pioneered teaching on such groundbreaking themes as generational curses, the biblical significance of Israel, and demonology.

Prince's radio program, which began in 1979, has been translated into more than a dozen languages and continues to touch lives. Derek's main gift of explaining the Bible and its teaching in a clear and simple way has helped build a foundation of faith in millions of lives. His nondenominational, nonsectarian approach has made his teaching equally relevant and helpful to people from all racial and religious backgrounds, and his teaching is estimated to have reached more than half the globe.

In 2002, he said, "It is my desire—and I believe the Lord's desire—that this ministry continue the work which God began through me over sixty years ago, until Jesus returns."

Derek Prince Ministries—International continues to reach out to believers in over 140 countries with Derek's teachings, fulfilling the mandate to keep on "until Jesus returns." This is accomplished through the outreaches of more than forty-five Derek Prince offices around the world, including primary work in Australia, Canada, China, France, Germany, the Netherlands, New Zealand, Norway, Russia, South Africa, Switzerland, the United Kingdom, and the United States. For current information about these and other worldwide locations, visit www.derekprince.com.